5

Grammar through text types

AF751580

PETER **DURKIN**
VIRGINIA **FERGUSON**

OXFORD
UNIVERSITY PRESS
AUSTRALIA & NEW ZEALAND

OXFORD
UNIVERSITY PRESS

Oxford University Press is a department of the University of Oxford. It furthers the University's objective of excellence in research, scholarship, and education by publishing worldwide. Oxford is a registered trademark of Oxford University Press in the UK and in certain other countries.

Published in Australia by
Oxford University Press
Level 8, 737 Bourke Street, Docklands, Victoria 3008, Australia

First published 2008
Reprinted 2010, 2011, 2012 (twice), 2013, 2014, 2015, 2016, 2017, 2018, 2019, 2020, 2021 (twice), 2022, 2023, 2024, 2025

ISBN 978 0 19 556040 4

MIX
Paper | Supporting responsible forestry
FSC® C043100
FSC www.fsc.org

Typeset Alice Graphics
Illustrated by Rob Mancini
Printed in India by Manipal Technologies Limited

Acknowledgments
The author and publisher wish to thank the following copyright holders for granting permission to reproduce their material.

Asch, Frank, 'Sunflakes', p. 12, © Frank Asch, first appeared in Country Pie, William Morrow & Company, New York, 1979; Fatchen, Max, 'Skateboard', p. 24, © Max Fatchen; Klein, Robin, 'How Nellie Patch Saved the Little Town of Wallabah', p. 57, © By arrangement with the Licensor, Robin Klein c/o Curtis Brown (Aust) Pty Ltd; Prevot, Jean-Marie/AUSCAPE, p. 26; Serraillier, Ian, 'The Visitor', p. 36, © Estate of Ian Serraillier First appeared in A Second Poetry Book, compiled by John Foster, OUP 1980.

Every effort has been made to trace the original source of copyright material contained in this book. The publisher would be pleased to hear from copyright holders to rectify any errors or omissions.

Contents

Introduction

Grammar Through Text Types uses factual and literary texts as the context for introducing basic grammar skills to primary school students:

Recount	Description	Exposition
Narrative	Explanation	Information Report
Poetry	Procedure	Transaction

The comprehensive range of grammatical conventions covered meets the requirements as outlined in the state and territory standards for primary schools.

The series consists of:

- Six workbooks with 30 double-page units covering a year's work at the relevant level
- A simple answer section located at the centre of the books
- Revision units that review important grammatical conventions at word, sentence and text level.

How to use this book

The *left-hand page* of each unit focuses on a particular grammatical convention within a specific text type.

The text sample for each unit has been chosen to provide:

- examples in context of the particular grammatical convention that is the focus of that unit
- a model of a particular text type that the students can then use as a basis for their own writing.

Left-hand page

Grammar focus

The left-hand column is used to highlight, in context, the particular grammatical feature.

Definition of grammatical feature

Activities related to the grammatical feature

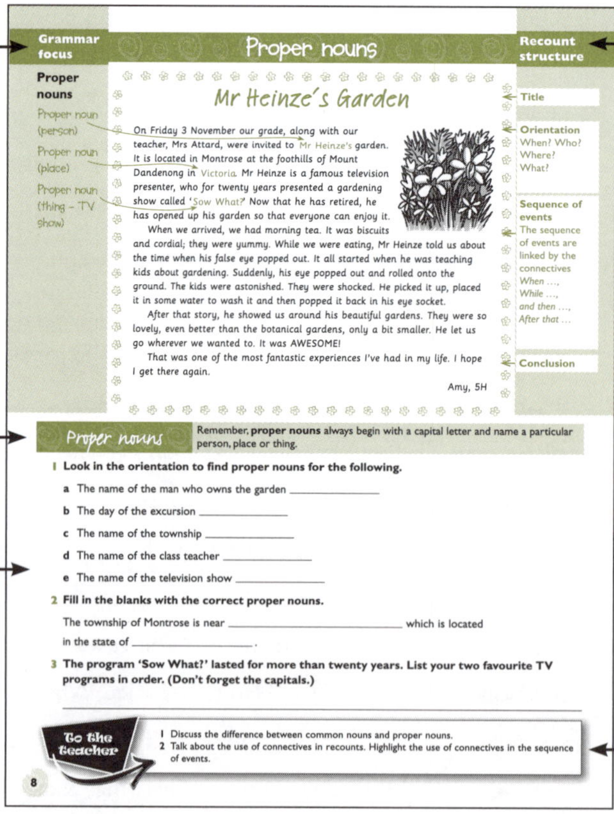

Grammar focus

Proper nouns

Recount structure

Proper nouns

Proper noun (person)

Proper noun (place)

Proper noun (thing – TV show)

Mr Heinze's Garden

On Friday 3 November our grade, along with our teacher, Mrs Attard, were invited to Mr Heinze's garden. It is located in Montrose at the foothills of Mount Dandenong in Victoria. Mr Heinze is a famous television presenter, who for twenty years presented a gardening show called 'Sow What?' Now that he has retired, he has opened up his garden so that everyone can enjoy it.

When we arrived, we had morning tea. It was biscuits and cordial; they were yummy. While we were eating, Mr Heinze told us about the time when his false eye popped out. It all started when he was teaching kids about gardening. Suddenly, his eye popped out and rolled onto the ground. The kids were astonished. They were shocked. He picked it up, placed it in some water to wash it and then popped it back in his eye socket.

After that story, he showed us around his beautiful gardens. They were so lovely, even better than the botanical gardens, only a bit smaller. He let us go wherever we wanted to. It was AWESOME!

That was one of the most fantastic experiences I've had in my life. I hope I get there again.

Amy, 5H

Title

Orientation
When? Who? Where? What?

Sequence of events
The sequence of events are linked by the connectives *When …, While …, and then …, After that …*

Conclusion

Proper nouns

Remember, **proper nouns** always begin with a capital letter and name a particular person, place or thing.

1 Look in the orientation to find proper nouns for the following.

a The name of the man who owns the garden ______________

b The day of the excursion ______________

c The name of the township ______________

d The name of the class teacher ______________

e The name of the television show ______________

2 Fill in the blanks with the correct proper nouns.

The township of Montrose is near ______________ which is located in the state of ______________ .

3 The program 'Sow What?' lasted for more than twenty years. List your two favourite TV programs in order. (Don't forget the capitals.)

____

To the teacher

1 Discuss the difference between common nouns and proper nouns.
2 Talk about the use of connectives in recounts. Highlight the use of connectives in the sequence of events.

8

Text type

The right-hand column is used to highlight the various features and structure of a particular text type.

A model for writing

A language model grounded in the relationship between text type and grammar

To the teacher

Advice and directions related to both the grammar and the text type

Introduction

The *right-hand page* of each unit provides practice in using the grammatical skills within and beyond that specific text type. As well, this page includes an engaging *Your turn to write* section, guiding the students as they apply the grammatical skills in their own writing of this particular text type.

Right-hand page

Unit number

Grammar focus examples and details

This provides examples of the grammar focus and a starting point for the activities that follow.

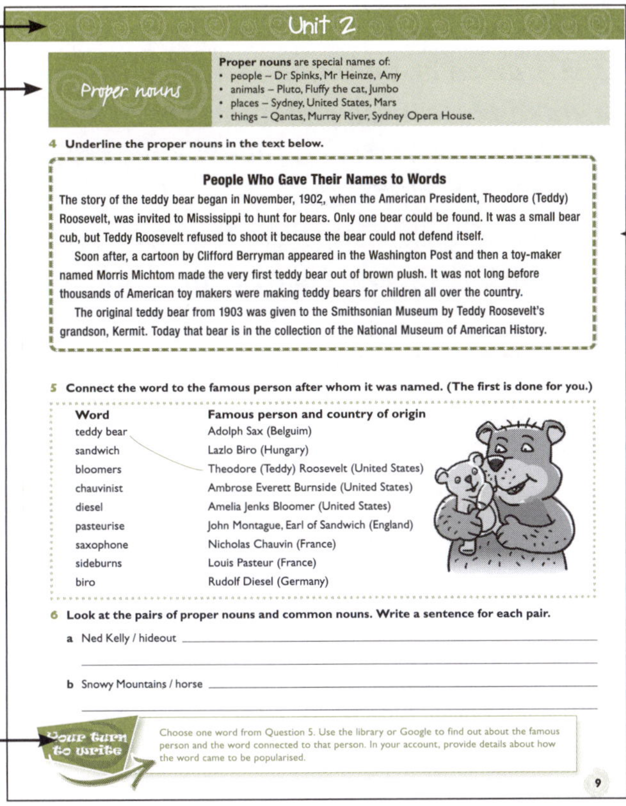

Unit 2

Proper nouns

Proper nouns are special names of:
- people – Dr Spinks, Mr Heinze, Amy
- animals – Pluto, Fluffy the cat, Jumbo
- places – Sydney, United States, Mars
- things – Qantas, Murray River, Sydney Opera House.

4 Underline the proper nouns in the text below.

People Who Gave Their Names to Words

The story of the teddy bear began in November, 1902, when the American President, Theodore (Teddy) Roosevelt, was invited to Mississippi to hunt for bears. Only one bear could be found. It was a small bear cub, but Teddy Roosevelt refused to shoot it because the bear could not defend itself.

Soon after, a cartoon by Clifford Berryman appeared in the Washington Post and then a toy-maker named Morris Michtom made the very first teddy bear out of brown plush. It was not long before thousands of American toy makers were making teddy bears for children all over the country.

The original teddy bear from 1903 was given to the Smithsonian Museum by Teddy Roosevelt's grandson, Kermit. Today that bear is in the collection of the National Museum of American History.

5 Connect the word to the famous person after whom it was named. (The first is done for you.)

Word	Famous person and country of origin
teddy bear	Adolph Sax (Belguim)
sandwich	Lazlo Biro (Hungary)
bloomers	Theodore (Teddy) Roosevelt (United States)
chauvinist	Ambrose Everett Burnside (United States)
diesel	Amelia Jenks Bloomer (United States)
pasteurise	John Montague, Earl of Sandwich (England)
saxophone	Nicholas Chauvin (France)
sideburns	Louis Pasteur (France)
biro	Rudolf Diesel (Germany)

6 Look at the pairs of proper nouns and common nouns. Write a sentence for each pair.

a Ned Kelly / hideout

b Snowy Mountains / horse

Your turn to write

Choose one word from Question 5. Use the library or Google to find out about the famous person and the word connected to that person. In your account, provide details about how the word came to be popularised.

9

Activities to further extend the specific grammar focus

The text on the previous page is used as the stimulus, but the activities on this page extend beyond that context.

Student's own writing

An off-the-page writing activity related to the text type and incorporating the grammatical feature treated in the unit

Self-assessment

The assessment section provides a summary of grammatical conventions used for each text type. Grammar is assessed within the text type to enable students to evaluate their ability to use language more effectively. The assessment section looks at:

- Text Purpose
- Text Structure
- Text Forms
- Grammatical features of the relevant text type.

Students can track their progress as they proceed through the units. The assessment section can be used in collaboration with the teacher to ascertain development of, and improvement in, the acquisition of grammar skills and the capacity to apply the grammatical conventions to write in the various text types.

Nouns

A noun is a naming word.

What a Scary Night!

Title

Orientation — When? Who? Where?

During the holidays I went to stay with my aunt. She has a holiday house way up high in the mountains.

noun (person) → aunt; noun (place) → mountains

Sequence of events

On the first night, I was tired so I went to bed early. I was a bit nervous. Outside, the moon was shining through the giant mountain ash trees. Their branches leaned right down, their shadows dancing outside the windows and their leaves swishing on the roof.

Just as my eyes started to close, all the possums on the mountain decided to have a ball on the roof. They scattered and scrunched and growled and grunted and thumped and jumped. It was a grand possum ball and it was just above my head. Suddenly, there was an enormous THUMP! A big brushy-tailed possum crashed through the skylight and landed on the floor right next to my nose. I shrieked, leapt out of bed and raced into my aunt's room and jumped into her bed. She was still in it!

noun (animal) → possums; noun (thing) → floor

The next morning we found the possum peeping out of a cupboard in the spare room. My aunt got it out of the door with a bamboo pole.

Personal comments

What a scary night that was for the start of my holidays!

by James, 5E

Nouns

A **common noun** is the ordinary name of something. For example, *aunt* (person); *mountains* (place); *possum* (animal); *floor* (thing)

An **abstract noun** names something that cannot be seen or heard or touched. For example, *fear, anger, love*

1 Look in the *orientation* above. Find the nouns.

a Someone who is your mother's or father's sister ____________

b The time when you don't go to work or school ____________

c Very high hills ____________

d A building where you live ____________

2 Find nouns for these clues in the *sequence of events*.

a a time when it is dark ____________ **b** a place to sleep ____________

c it shines at night ____________ **d** tall plants with leaves ____________

3 Look at the *conclusion*. List two nouns. ____________ ____________

To the teacher

1 Recounts also feature past-tense action verbs (*growled, grunted*). Highlight these in the text above and provide opportunities for the students to include them in their own recounts.
2 Use a highlighter to mark nouns in the sequence of events.

Nouns

A **common noun** is the name of any general thing. Common nouns never start with a capital letter, unless they begin a sentence.

Abstract nouns refer to a quality, feeling or condition. For instance, *biscuit* is not an abstract noun because we can see it and touch it. *Love* is an abstract noun because it is a feeling that we cannot see or touch.

4 Add to the common nouns in the boxes by:

a finding at least one word in the recount opposite to go under each heading

b adding nouns of your own under each heading.

Parts of the body	Parts of a house	Animals	Plants	Furniture

5 Circle the common noun in each pair.

tired | possums

bed | raced

shadows | down

suddenly | morning

scattered | ball

mountains | jumped

room | their

windows | on

shrieked | nose

thumps | night

just | head

has | cupboard

6 Write the abstract nouns in sentences of your own.

a beauty ______________________________

b bravery ______________________________

c fear ______________________________

Sometimes an abstract noun can be formed by adding a suffix. For example, *kind* + *ness* = *kindness; free* + *dom* = *freedom*

7 Add the suffix to the words to form abstract nouns. (Be careful! Sometimes the base word is changed when the suffix is added.)

a Add *-ness* kind ____________ happy ____________ silly ____________

b Add *-ism* hero ____________ patriot ____________ sensational ____________

c Add *-ance* tolerate ____________ guide ____________ annoy ____________

Your turn to write

Write a recount about a time when you were scared or in danger. Before you begin, plan your recount.

1 The orientation: Jot some notes about who, when, where, what.

2 The sequence of events: Write about what happens in the order that it happened.

3 Think about how it all ended, and write a few notes for the conclusion.

Proper nouns

Proper noun (person)

Proper noun (place)

Proper noun (thing – TV show)

Mr Heinze's Garden

On Friday 3 November our grade, along with our teacher, Mrs Attard, were invited to Mr Heinze's garden. It is located in Montrose at the foothills of Mount Dandenong in Victoria. Mr Heinze is a famous television presenter, who for twenty years presented a gardening show called 'Sow What?' Now that he has retired, he has opened up his garden so that everyone can enjoy it.

When we arrived, we had morning tea. It was biscuits and cordial; they were yummy. While we were eating, Mr Heinze told us about the time when his false eye popped out. It all started when he was teaching kids about gardening. Suddenly, his eye popped out and rolled onto the ground. The kids were astonished. They were shocked. He picked it up, placed it in some water to wash it and then popped it back in his eye socket.

After that story, he showed us around his beautiful gardens. They were so lovely, even better than the botanical gardens, only a bit smaller. He let us go wherever we wanted to. It was AWESOME!

That was one of the most fantastic experiences I've had in my life. I hope I get there again.

Amy, 5H

Title

Orientation
When? Who? Where? What?

Sequence of events
The sequence of events are linked by the connectives *When …, While …, and then …, After that …*

Conclusion

Proper nouns

Remember, **proper nouns** always begin with a capital letter and name a particular person, place or thing.

1 Look in the orientation to find proper nouns for the following.

a The name of the man who owns the garden ________________

b The day of the excursion ________________

c The name of the township ________________

d The name of the class teacher ________________

e The name of the television show ________________

2 Fill in the blanks with the correct proper nouns.

The township of Montrose is near ________________________________ which is located in the state of ______________________ .

3 The program 'Sow What?' lasted for more than twenty years. List your two favourite TV programs in order. (Don't forget the capitals.)

____

To the teacher

1 Discuss the difference between common nouns and proper nouns.
2 Talk about the use of connectives in recounts. Highlight the use of connectives in the sequence of events.

Proper nouns

Proper nouns are special names of:
- people – Dr Spinks, Mr Heinze, Amy
- animals – Pluto, Fluffy the cat, Jumbo
- places – Sydney, United States, Mars
- things – Qantas, Murray River, Sydney Opera House.

4 Underline the proper nouns in the text below.

People Who Gave Their Names to Words

The story of the teddy bear began in November, 1902, when the American President, Theodore (Teddy) Roosevelt, was invited to Mississippi to hunt for bears. Only one bear could be found. It was a small bear cub, but Teddy Roosevelt refused to shoot it because the bear could not defend itself.

Soon after, a cartoon by Clifford Berryman appeared in the Washington Post and then a toy-maker named Morris Michtom made the very first teddy bear out of brown plush. It was not long before thousands of American toy makers were making teddy bears for children all over the country.

The original teddy bear from 1903 was given to the Smithsonian Museum by Teddy Roosevelt's grandson, Kermit. Today that bear is in the collection of the National Museum of American History.

5 Connect the word to the famous person after whom it was named. (The first is done for you.)

Word	Famous person and country of origin
teddy bear	Adolph Sax (Belguim)
sandwich	Lazlo Biro (Hungary)
bloomers	Theodore (Teddy) Roosevelt (United States)
chauvinist	Ambrose Everett Burnside (United States)
diesel	Amelia Jenks Bloomer (United States)
pasteurise	John Montague, Earl of Sandwich (England)
saxophone	Nicholas Chauvin (France)
sideburns	Louis Pasteur (France)
biro	Rudolf Diesel (Germany)

6 Look at the pairs of proper nouns and common nouns. Write a sentence for each pair.

a Ned Kelly / hideout ______________________________

____

b Snowy Mountains / horse ______________________________

____

Your turn to write

Choose one word from Question 5. Use the library or Google to find out about the famous person and the word connected to that person. In your account, provide details about how the word came to be popularised.

Collective nouns

The Crowded House

Title

Orientation: When? Who? Where?

A long time ago there was a man named Joseph. He lived in an old cottage with his wife and three little daughters. His cottage contained three rooms: a kitchen, a bedroom for himself and his wife and one for his daughters.

Every morning when it was time for work, he would go out, chop wood and sell it just to keep his family alive. All the rich people would drive past in their horses and carts, going to their massive houses.

Complication

One day Joseph, his wife and his daughters got sick of this life. The next day Joseph went to see the Wise Man. He had long hair and wore a black cloak.

Sequence of events

He knocked on the Wise Man's door. "Come in," he said. "What is your problem?"

Joseph replied, "I'm fed up with my life. My house is tiny and we hardly have any room to move."

"Hmm," said the Wise Man. "Can you please bring your chickens into the house?" So Joseph went home and told his wife. They had twenty chickens. The whole brood went inside.

a group of chickens

A week later, Joseph went back to the Wise Man and told him how bad it was. The Wise Man said, "Bring in your cows." So Joseph went home and brought in his herd of cows. It was a madhouse. Again he went back to the Wise Man, who said, "Bring in some birds." And so it went on. In went a litter of pups, a team of horses and a gaggle of geese. The house was exploding with animals.

a group of geese

Joseph could stand it no longer. Once more he went back to the Wise Man, who declared, "LET EVERYTHING OUT." And everything went out.

Resolution

Now the house was quiet and each room seemed huge. Everything was fantastic, and Joseph and his family never complained again.

Coda: shows what has been learnt

Moral: Be thankful for what you have.

Retold by Nova

Nouns

Collective nouns stand for a collection of things. For example, *a brood of chickens* is a group or collection of chickens.

1 Look in the text to find collective nouns to describe these groups.

a ______________ of pups   a ______________ of horses   a ______________ of geese

a ______________ of chickens   a ______________ of cows

2 Find a collective noun to describe a group of people who are related. ______________

To the teacher

Nouns for collections of animals can be unusual. We could just use one word, like *mob* or *flock* for every group, but there are many different words to describe animal groups, for example, a *nest* of mice. See how many more the students can generate.

Unit 3

Animate and Inanimate Collective Nouns

Animate means *living*: for example, animals and people.

a litter of kittens

Inanimate means *not living*.

a flight of stairs

3 In the box are collective nouns for inanimate things. Match the collective noun to each group of things.

Collective Nouns

bunch, forest, pack, suit, batch, chest, library

a ______________ of trees

a ______________ of cards

a ______________ of clothes

a ______________ of books

a ______________ of flowers

a ______________ of drawers

a ______________ of cakes

4 Below is a list of collective nouns and groups. Use the list to find the collective nouns in the word search.

- a brood of chickens
- a collection of stamps
- a flock of birds
- a school of whales
- a choir of singers
- a crew of sailors
- a hedge of bushes
- a plague of mice
- a posse of sheriff's men
- a flight of aeroplanes
- a litter of kittens
- a pack of wolves
- a punnet of strawberries
- a swarm of bees

S	M	N	F	L	O	C	K	R	S
C	D	O	V	V	W	P	E	W	M
H	O	I	B	E	U	T	A	Z	U
O	O	T	R	N	T	R	F	S	C
O	R	C	N	I	M	V	S	S	K
L	B	E	L	P	L	A	G	U	E
P	T	L	P	K	L	T	S	E	N
A	D	L	J	C	E	G	D	E	H
C	H	O	I	R	P	O	S	S	E
K	I	C	T	H	G	I	L	F	P

Your turn to write

Write your own story with a moral. It could be a retelling of a well-known story or fable, or it could be your own narrative. Make sure you include the orientation, a complication, a sequence of events and a resolution.

Compound nouns

Grammar focus

Compound nouns

Sunlight is a compound noun.

Sun + light = **sunlight**

Snowflake is a compound noun.

Snow + flake = **snowflake**

Sunflakes

If sunlight fell like snowflakes,
gleaming yellow and so bright,
we could build a sunman,
we could have a sunball fight,
we could watch the sunflakes
drifting in the sky.
We could go sleighing
in the middle of July
through sundrifts and sunbanks,
we could ride a sunmobile,
and we could touch sunflakes –
I wonder how they'd feel.

Frank Asch

Poetry structure

Title
This poem uses repetition and rhyme.

- Find the words which are repeated.
- Circle the words which rhyme with: *bright* *sky* *sunmobile*.

Poet

Nouns — **Compound nouns** are formed by putting two nouns together to form a new word. For example, *snow* + *ball* = *snowball*

1 **Many of the compound nouns in the poem begin with *sun*. List them.**

__________ __________ __________ __________

__________ __________

2 **One compound noun begins with the word *snow*. Write it.** __________

3 **Fill the boxes with as many compound nouns as you can.**

sunman snowman

Compound nouns beginning with *snow*	Compound nouns beginning with *sun*
snowman	**sunshine**

To the teacher

1 Talk to the students about poetic licence. Often a poet will make up words to conjure up pictures in the reader's mind. Words such as *sunflakes* and *sunball* are not in the dictionary, but they create vivid images for the reader.
2 Reread the poem with the students several times. What do they like about the poem?

Unit 4

Hyphens

The hyphen is a small dash that shows that two or more words belong together. Some compound nouns are joined together by hyphens. For example, *sister-in-law; twenty-one*

There are three kinds of compound nouns.

1 Two words joined together, e.g. sunlight, moonshine

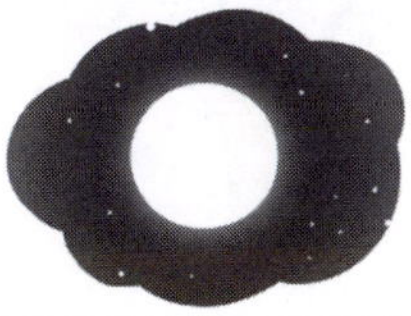

2 Two separate words, e.g. tiger snake

3 Two words linked by a hyphen, e.g. bumble-bee, three-year-old

4 Classify the nouns in the box under their correct headings

six-pack	weekend	second cousin	hairbrush	swagman	man-eater
red-hot	stingray	wood-shed	ground floor	space shuttle	bathroom
half-sister	apple tree	three-year-old	pea-shooter		

Two words joined together	Two separate words	Two words joined by a hyphen

5 Draw pictures to show the difference in these headings.

FOUR-YEAR-OLD pet saved from drowning	FOUR YEAR-OLD pets saved from drowning

Your turn to write

Use a spare sheet of paper. Brainstorm as many ideas as you can about the topic *Sun* or *Snow*. Select a title. Arrange your words into lines. Write a poem!

Pronouns are words that take the place of nouns.

The Fox and the Stork – a Fable

Title

Orientation Who? What?

One day a fox invited a stork to dinner. The fox was a mean creature, and all they had to eat was some thin soup in a shallow dish.

Complication

The fox quickly gobbled his soup, but the poor stork couldn't get a mouthful in her long, narrow bill. She tried again and again, but she was still as hungry at the end of dinner as she had been at the beginning.

She is a pronoun. It takes the place of the noun **stork**.

Sequence of events

"Don't you like my lovely soup?" asked the fox. "Come on, surely you could eat a little more than that!"

"I'm sure it was very tasty," said the stork, "but I cannot lap food up like cats or dogs or foxes do!"

The next week the stork invited the fox to dinner.

"Thank you for your kind invitation," he said when he arrived.

He is a pronoun. It takes the place of the noun **fox**.

The stork smiled as she handed him a long, thin jar full of milk and honey. It had a wonderful smell.

The stork thrust her long bill into the jar and quickly ate every bit of her meal, but the fox couldn't even get his tongue inside. He had to make do by licking the outside of the jar, and he was starving!

Resolution

"Well, now you've paid me back," said the fox. "You couldn't eat my dinner, and I couldn't eat yours. Fair's fair!"

Pronouns

Pronouns are usually small words which are used in place of nouns. Without pronouns our language would be very stilted.

Imagine: *The fox was hungry so the fox made soup, but the fox wouldn't share it.*

Instead of: *The fox was hungry so he made soup, but he wouldn't share it.*

Personal pronouns are words that are used in place of persons or things

1 Read the fable above again. Circle the personal pronouns in the box that also appear in the fable.

2 List the personal pronouns which are left over.

________ ________ ________ ________

3 Write pronouns to replace the underlined words.

The stork couldn't get a mouthful in her long narrow bill. The stork ________ tried again and again, but the stork ________ was still as hungry at the end of the dinner as the stork ________ had been at the beginning.

Personal pronouns

I	we	me	us
you	he	she	it
they	him	them	

To the teacher

Look again at the fable with the students. Notice how the pronouns keep referring back to the main characters, the fox and the stork. Pronouns such as *he, she, you* are used in the text to refer back to something which has already been mentioned. In this way, the text is much more cohesive and readable.

Possessive pronouns

Possessive pronouns take the place of nouns that are owned by someone or something.

That jar is *mine*.

That tongue is *hers*.

4 Use possessive pronouns from the box to write sentences showing possession.

Possessive pronouns

mine ours yours hers his its theirs

a The soup belongs to me.

The soup is mine.

b The milk belongs to you.

____

c The dogs belong to us.

____

d The tickets belong to them.

____

5 Look in both the personal and the possessive pronoun boxes. Write pronouns in the correct groups below.

Pronouns about yourself

I

______
______
______

Pronouns about females

She

______
______
______

Pronouns about males

him

______
______
______

Pronouns about others

them

______
______
______

6 Write a word that rhymes with each of these pronouns. Include the rhyming pairs in sentences together. For example, us – bus; He helped us onto the bus.

a he ______________________________

b mine ______________________________

c him ______________________________

d it ______________________________

Your turn to write

Pronouns such as *I*, *me* are called first-person pronouns. Write a story or a fable in the first person. You could retell a fable or a fairy tale beginning "My name is Little Red Riding Hood and one day I decided to go for a stroll in the woods". Or you could be the hare in "The Hare and the Tortoise".

Grammar focus

Noun plurals

Information report structure

Plurals

rhinoceros can be used for singular or plural.

grass can be used for singular or plural.

fingernails is the plural of fingernail.

Greater Indian One-horned Rhinoceros

← Title

The greater Indian one-horned rhinoceros is one of the world's largest rhinoceros. Unlike other rhinoceros, it has only one horn.

← Classifying statement

Where It Lives

The rhinoceros lives in Nepal and Eastern India. It is solitary in nature and spends hours wallowing in mud or water, or feeding on grass.

← Series of facts
The facts are organised into paragraphs.

Appearance and Habits

The rhino, like the hippo, is a large, fearsome animal which is equally at home in the water as it is on land. It has few natural enemies. It can run up to 60 kilometres per hour, has a thick armour-like skin and it lives in lonely, isolated areas.

Endangered Species

Despite all this, it has almost been wiped out. This is because it is hunted for its horn.

The rhino's horn is made of keratin, the same substance as our fingernails. People believe that rhino horn powder makes strong medicine. They believe that jewellery and daggers made from the horn will give the owners special powers.

The rhinoceros is not the only animal in danger. Whales, cheetahs, tigers, elephants, gorillas and many birds are among the species threatened because of the actions of human beings.

← Concluding statement

Plural nouns

A **singular noun** is just one of something. The noun *dagger* is singular. It means *one dagger*.

A **plural noun** means more than one. The noun *daggers* is plural. It means *more than one dagger*.

1 Write the plurals for six different animals in the text.

____

____

2 Find and circle the plural for the noun *enemy*. Write the plurals for these words.

army __________ city __________ party __________ body __________

3 In the report above, circle the word *jewellery*. It has no singular form. Write it in a sentence.

____

To the teacher

Look again at the structure of the information report. The classifying statement always introduces the topic and often involves a classification of the thing about which the report is written. The main body of the report consists of facts and diagrams about the topic.

Plural nouns

When forming plurals, some nouns need to be changed or added to. Some stay the same.

For words ending in ch, sh, ss, or x add **es**, e.g. bush–bushes.

4 Write the plurals for these nouns.

a fox ______ lynx ______ ass ______

b ostrich ______ brush ______ watch ______

When a word ends in y following a vowel, simply add **s**, e.g. valley–valleys.

c donkey ______ boy ______

toy ______ monkey ______

For most words ending in f or fe, change to **ves**, e.g wolf–wolves.

d shelf ______ calf ______

knife ______ loaf ______

5 Write the singular for these nouns:

a tomatoes ______

heroes ______

For most words ending in o add **es**, e.g. potato–potatoes.

For words ending in y following a consonant, change the y to i and add **es** to form the plural e.g. fly–flies.

b flies ______ families ______

injuries ______

6 Write the plurals for these two shortened words from the information report.

hippo ______ rhino ______

7 Circle the correct plural in each pair.

a scissor / scissors **b** deer / deers

c moose's / moose **d** trout / trouts

e geese / gooses **f** tooths / teeth

g mouses / mice **h** trouser / trousers

We form some plurals by changing the base word. Other words do not change to form the plural, e.g. sheep–sheep.

8 Change these words into plurals and write them in sentences.

a thief ______

b mousetrap ______

Your turn to write

The snow leopard and Siberian tiger are among endangered animal species. Select one of these, or another animal of your choice, and write an information report about it. When you are researching for facts about your animal, focus on why it is in danger of extinction.

Revision

Common nouns

A **common noun** is the ordinary name for people, places, animals and things.

1 Write the names.

a three types of insects ____________ ____________ ____________

b the ingredients for a sandwich ______________________________

c four cooking implements ____________ ____________ ____________ ____________

2 Circle the common nouns.

blanket	car	try	doll	fingers	hippo	ring	jumped	red	angrily
pie	sun	paper	shark	jaws	cry	flour	arrow	baby	

3 Write the plural forms of the nouns and then number them in alphabetical order.

☐ branch ____________	☐ fox ____________	☐ radish ____________
☐ boss ____________	☐ party ____________	☐ city ____________
☐ donkey ____________	☐ thief ____________	☐ wolf ____________
☐ wife ____________	☐ potato ____________	☐ tomato ____________

Abstract nouns

Abstract nouns name something that cannot be seen or heard or touched, e.g. fair, love, enjoyment.

4 Form abstract nouns by adding suffixes to the words in the boxes.

-ness	
sick	
happy	
lazy	
sad	

-tion	
attract	
admire	
explain	
distract	

-ment	
enjoy	
appoint	
encourage	
judge	

5 Highlight the abstract nouns.

truth	john	car	sadness	carried	foot
bravery	clothes	his	freedom	justice	exhaustion
fare	fairness	curious	silly	jokes	conclusion

Proper nouns

Proper nouns have a capital letter.
Proper nouns are the names of particular people, places and things.

6 The article below is about survival in a snake pit. The capital letters for all the proper nouns have been changed. Use a red pen. Write capital letters in the correct places.

Snakes

peter snyman spent fifty days in a small glass and brick cage in a snake park near johannesburg, south africa, with twenty-four of the world's deadliest snakes. He had a break of 20 minutes outside the cage each day, but otherwise he spent every minute with his companions – six black mambas, six egyptian cobras, six puff adders and six boomslangs (tree snakes). He came out on 27 may 1979 and said: "Thank god that's over. I couldn't have taken another day." The snakes said nothing.

Collective nouns

Collective nouns stand for a group or a collection of things.

7 Complete the collective nouns below with words from the box.

brood herd litter school flock pack swarm fleet library bunch

a a ____________ of bees **b** a ____________ of wolves

c a ____________ of kittens **d** a ____________ of hens

e a ____________ of ships **f** a ____________ of books

g a ____________ of birds **h** a ____________ of whales

i a ____________ of bananas **j** a ____________ of cattle

Now write these two collective nouns in sentences.

k team ____

l band ____

Compound nouns

Compound nouns are formed by putting two nouns together to form a new word.

8 Add nouns from Group B to nouns from Group A to form compound nouns.

Group A	
gang	birth
play	rain
snow	sting
sun	air

Group B	
day	storm
ball	ray
set	port
time	plank

gangplank ____________

____________ ____________

____________ ____________

____________ ____________

Adjectives tell us more about nouns

Being Blind at School

Title

Introduction Tells what is being described

My name is Brent and I am blind.

When I first went to school, everyone wanted to use my guide cane. They pretended they were blind and went staggering all around the school. I only let my best friends use it now.

Characteristic features Describes details about the subject

descriptive adjective → Reading is my favourite subject. The blind school supplies Braille books for me so that I can read almost anything I like. The hardest part is trying to use a dictionary. It is a big, thick dictionary. It consists of seventy-two ← *numbering adjective* heavy volumes, each about fifteen centimetres thick. When they are stacked up on top of each other, they nearly reach the roof!

I like cricket and riding my two-wheeled bike best. I can hear the ball bouncing and I hit it when it comes close. And I can tell where I am riding by listening to the sound that the wind makes against the picket fences.

Final comment Personal comment about the subject

quantitative adjective → Even though I can't do everything that my friends can do, there are some things that I can do that other kids can't. For instance, when mum says it's time for bed, I can read until midnight. I don't need a light, so who's to know the difference?

Adjectives

There are many different kinds of adjectives. **Descriptive adjectives** tell us *what kind of* about the noun: for example, *favourite* subject. **Numbering adjectives** tell us *how many*, for example, *seventy two* volumes. **Quantitative adjectives** tell us *how much*, for example, *some* things.

1 Read the description above, and write adjectives used for these nouns.

________ friends ________ things ________ part

________, ________ dictionary ________ bike ________ fences

2 Use the adjectives in brackets in sentences of your own.

a (heavy) ________________

b (fifty-two) ________________

c (few) ________________

To the teacher

Descriptions often contain a variety of adjectives to evaluate and classify. They also contain adjectival phrases, which are introduced with a preposition.

Adjectives

Adjectives can tell us about **colour**, **shape**, **how many** and **how much**.

3 Look first at the cartoon of the principal. Then match the nouns in Box A, with the adjectives in Box B, to best describe him.

A

a ______________ sleeves

b ______________ eyebrows

c ______________ teeth

d ______________ head

e ______________ ears

f ______________ principal

g ______________ eyes

B

bald
huge
angry
tiny
patchy
white
bushy

4 Use the adjectives and the noun in the boxes to make interesting sentences of your own. (One example is done for you.)

a adjectives → large sailing white sleek powerful | noun → ship

We watched the large, sleek, white, sailing ship float by.

b adjectives → glossy, sports, racy, red | noun → car

____

c adjectives → sweet delicious rich | noun → cake

____

d adjectives → ancient wrinkly red tall gnarled | noun → gum

____

Adjectives

We can sometimes form adjectives by adding suffixes to the word.
For example, *y*, *al*, *ous* or *ful* can be added to the end of a noun.
The weather was icy (ice+y); James Cook is famous (fame+ous)

5 Complete the table by forming the adjectives. Use a dictionary to check; some are tricky!

(noun) + ful	(noun)+ y	(noun)+ ous
thought + ful =	cloud + y =	danger + ous =
care + ful =	wind + y =	marvel + ous =
help + ful =	sun + y =	mountain + ous =
waste + ful =	fog + y =	adventure + ous =

Your turn to write

Who is someone you admire? Write a description of this person. In your introduction state what particular quality it is that you admire. Then provide some descriptive details about the person.

Comparing adjectives

Dare-devil Durkin

Title

Orientation: Who? When? Where? What?

When I was nine I lived on a dairy farm. My brother and sister and I loved to play in the home paddock where there were three huge chestnut trees.

Sequence of events

Our favourite game was climbing into the tallest tree, standing on a springy branch, leaping through the air to catch another one, swinging on that one, and so on, until we reached the ground. I thought I was so good – the best. I thought I was even better than Tarzan! I called myself "Dare-devil Durkin".

comparing adjective (tallest)

One time though, I learnt a hard lesson. I stood on the highest branch, leapt through the air, and grabbed the next branch. It broke! I hurtled through the air, plunged towards the ground and landed – CRASH! – flat on my back. I survived, but I was the sickest, sorriest dare-devil that had ever climbed a tree.

comparing adjective (sickest)

Conclusion

After that, I didn't feel like the bravest dare-devil any longer, just the silliest.

Writer

Peter D.

Adjectives

Comparing adjectives enable us to compare two or more things. Comparing adjectives usually end in *-er* when comparing two things. They end in *-est* when comparing more than two things. (For example *tall, taller, tallest*). These comparing adjectives are sometimes called "Adjectives of degree".

1 Circle the comparing adjectives in the text.

2 Include adjectives in brackets in sentences of your own.

a (scary) ______________________

b (scarier) ______________________

c (scariest) ______________________

3 Fill the gaps in the boxes.

little	less	least
good	________	best
bad	worse	________

silly	sillier	silliest
sorry	________	________
________	braver	________

To the teacher

1 Revise the recount structure. Note how in the orientation much information about who, when, where, what can be introduced with very few words. Also point out the use of time connectives in the sequence of events, for example, *when …, one time …, after that …*
2 Revise the different types of adjectives: descriptive, comparing, etc.

Some adjectives use *more* or *most* instead of adding *-er* or *-est*.

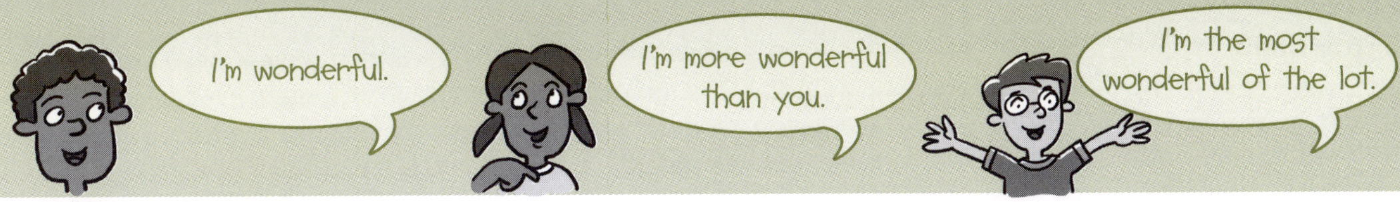

4 Complete the table.

delicious	more delicious	most delicious
disgusting	______________	most disgusting
______________	more wonderful	______________
beautiful	______________	______________

5 Look at the picture and then use the word bank to fill the gaps.

more taller most smaller smallest tallest

a The elephant is ______________ than the kangaroo.

b The frog is ______________ than the koala.

c The giraffe is the ______________ animal of all.

d The mouse is ______________ timid than the lion.

e The lion is the ______________ ferocious animal.

f The frog is the ______________ of them all.

6 Use this word in a sentence.

huge ____

____

7 Highlight the best comparing adjective in each sentence.

a The home paddock is (small / smaller / smallest) than the back paddock.

b That was the (worst / bad / worse) fall I ever had.

c The (big / bigger / biggest) tree has the (many / more / most) chestnuts of all the trees.

d Our teacher is the (more entertaining / most entertaining) teacher in the school.

e I am the (fast / faster / fastest) runner in my class.

Your turn to write

Write a recount about yourself. Choose one of these titles for your topic: "The most adventurous thing that happened to me" or "The most dangerous thing that happened to me" or "The scariest thing that happened to me".

Action verbs
are doing words

action verbs

There are more than 20 action verbs in the poem.
How many can you find?

Skateboard

We **twist**
and we **turn**
and the pavement
we **burn**
as we rocket
downhill at a rate.
We **whoop**
and we **swoop**
as we **crouch**
and we **stoop**
on the board
where we **ride**
when we **skate**.
With a shove
and a run
it is furious fun
as we **roll**
with a sweep
and a swerve.
Then we **reel**
and we **rip**
in a breathtaking trip
while keeping
our balance
and nerve.
We **swing**
and we **sway**
in a dare-devil way
on a hair-raising,
zig-zagging track.
Our father
once **tried**.
You'll find him
inside
with a very
large bruise
on his back.

Max Fatchen

Poems can take different shapes.
This is a *concrete poem*. (It twists and turns like a skateboard.)
You could write a concrete poem.
First, think of a subject.
Second, think of a shape.
Third, brainstorm lots of action verbs about the subject.
Fourth, write your poem.

Example: High Jump

We start
with a skip
then we trot
and run towards
the high bar.
We jump over the bar and
p l u n g e d o w n
to crash
in the
SAND.

1 Look again at the poem to find action words that rhyme with the words below.

rate ________________ mist________________ hide ________________

2 Write five action words which begin with the 'r' sound.

____

3 Find two action words to describe how we bend on a skateboard.

____

When words begin with the same letters or sounds in a line, it is called alliteration.

To the teacher

The poem provides the perfect opportunity to exemplify the action words through mime. In pairs, as a group, or as a class, mime the different skateboard actions as the teacher or a class member reads the poem.

Verbs

Verbs are action, saying, sensing or relating verbs. Every sentence has a verb.

take	leap	sprint	move	run	dodge
shake	fly	launch	slip	give	look
strain	explode	drive	splash	blow	play

4 Fill the containers with action verbs which describe what we do when playing sports. (Choose words from the box above, and add more of your own.)

On a skate board	On the basketball court	In the swimming pool	On the athletics track
twist turn	________	________	________
roll skate swing	________	________	________
sway	________	________	________
	________	________	________
	________	________	________
	________	________	________

said	cried	screamed	continued	replied
responded	shouted	whispered	denied	claimed
pleaded	stammered	gasped	explained	suggested
reported	murmured	asked	told	sighed

5 Sometimes you can choose a different saying verb to add meaning or interest to your writing. Circle the most suitable word in each of the boxes.

Mario and his friend walked down the street. "Let's go in that old house," he [pleaded / said / suggested].

There were no lights. He [shouted / called / cried] out but no one answered. Something grabbed him by the shoulder.

He [exclaimed / shouted / screamed] with fright. Then he turned. "Quick!" he [murmured / said / whispered]. "Let's get out of here!"

He looked at his friend. He was as white as a ghost. "That was close," he [gasped / said / sighed].

Helping verbs

Compound verbs

drink: simple verb

creep: simple verb

are: (helping verb) + surprised: (main verb) = are surprised: (compound verb)

Why Are People Frightened of Vampire Bats?

Title

Identifying statement
What is being explained

People are frightened of vampire bats because they drink blood to live.

Explanation sequence

The normal prey of vampire bats is cattle. To feed, the bats creep up on their prey. Their razor-sharp front teeth are used to cut away the skin of their victims. After they have bitten into the flesh, they lap up the blood with their tongues.

razor sharp front teeth

Diagram

Horror movies have shown bats as large, terrifying animals, but when they see them, people are surprised. Their wingspan is only 20 centimetres and their body is the size of a person's thumb.

There is one good reason, however, why people should watch out for vampire bats. They carry a deadly virus called rabies.

Concluding statement

So vampire bats can be dangerous, but they are not like the horror creatures from Dracula. They feed on the blood of animals. They do not return from the dead to suck the blood from the throats of innocent people.

Verbs

A **simple verb** contains only one word.
For example: They *drink* blood. (The verb is *drink*.)
Bats *creep* up on their prey (The verb is *creep*.)
A **compound verb** contains more than one word.
For example: Their teeth *are used* to bite. (*are* + *used* = two verbs)
After they *have bitten* ... (*have* + *bitten* = two verbs)
A compound verb is made up of a helping verb such as *have* and a main verb such as *bitten*.

1 Highlight all the simple action verbs you can find in the text.

2 Find and write two compound verbs beginning with the helping word *have*.

____

3 Write the compound verb in a sentence of your own.

are surprised ______________________________

To the teacher

1 Look at the structure of an explanation. Note that the title of an explanation often takes the form of a question, which indicates what the explanation is about.
2 Explanations usually contain present-tense action verbs and helping (auxiliary) verbs.

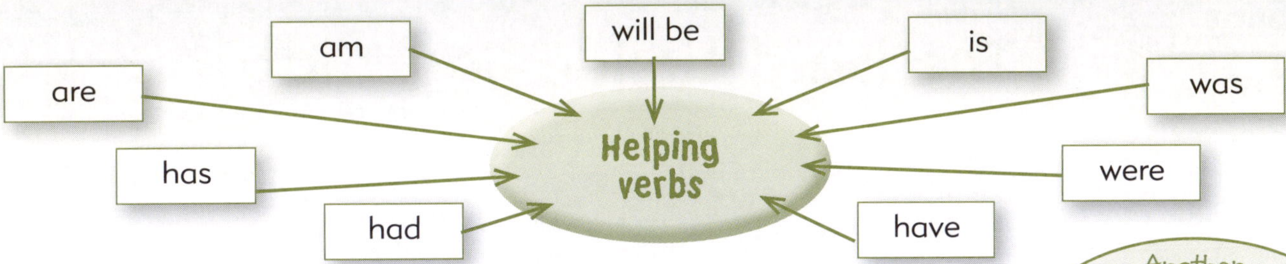

4 **Choose suitable helping verbs for these sentences. Then draw a box around all the compound verbs in the sentences.**

a I ______ eaten my play lunch and now I ______ going to play netball.

b Yesterday the school bus ______ stopped at the crossing.

c I ______ be playing netball on Saturday.

d Our teacher ______ forgotten that it's lunch time.

e We ______ going on an excursion tomorrow.

5 **Complete your own verb sums by filling the gaps.**

helping verb + action verb = compound verb				
were	+	chosen	=	were chosen
am	+	______	=	am racing
was	+	______	=	was bitten
have	+	changed	=	______
are	+	chasing	=	______
will be	+	______	=	will be punished

E	V	A	H	I
E	S	H	A	S
D	R	J	R	W
A	V	E	E	A
H	A	M	W	S

6 **Complete the helping verb word search and then use the verbs you have found to complete the sentences.**

a We ______ found the lost money.

b The letter ______ posted yesterday.

c After dinner we ______ ready.

d I ______ trying to write neatly.

e The teacher ______ watching you.

Your turn to write

Use the library, the Internet or books of your own to conduct research of animals or mythical beasts which have frightened people over the years. When you have chosen a topic, write an explanation telling why people have been frightened. The title of your explanation might be "Why people have been frightened by (sabre-toothed tigers / Minotaurs / hydras / werewolves)...".

Present-tense verbs

In this procedure many of the present tense verbs begin the sentences.

The Hard-boiled Egg Trick

Materials

2 hard-boiled eggs (Make sure they are well cooked.)
a chair

What to do

1 Place a hard-boiled egg on a chair. Don't let your audience see you do this.
2 Sit on the egg carefully. (Don't use a raw egg, or you know what will happen.)
3 Take the other hard-boiled egg. Show it to your audience.
4 Pretend to put it in your mouth.
5 Puff your cheeks out as though you have an egg in there. (What you really do is keep the egg in your hand.)
6 Make loud swallowing noises. Show a lot of effort. (Make the audience think you really have swallowed the egg.)
7 While they are watching your face, slip the egg into your pocket without moving your arm too much.
8 Suddenly, stop grunting and stand up, looking very relieved.
9 Point to the chair with the egg sitting on it.

You have laid an egg and it is already cooked!

Highlight all the present-tense verbs.

How many can you find?

Goal
The goal is stated in the title.

Materials
The materials needed to achieve the goal

Steps
The steps are numbered in order.

Verb tenses

Once we know what the action is, we want to know when the action took place. This is called the tense of a verb. There are three basic tenses: present, past and future.

Present tense (now): I *sit* on the chair.

Past tense (already happened): I *sat* on the chair.

Future tense (it is yet to happen): I *will sit* on the chair.

1 List the present-tense verbs that are used to begin sentences in the procedure.

____

____

To the teacher

1 Note that in future tense, the main verb often requires another verb to help it to become an action in the future, for example, "I *will* sit on the chair." (The word *will* is the helping verb.)
2 Talk about the structure of a procedure. Note that the present-tense verbs at the beginning of each instruction often take the form of a command, for example, *Place, Sit*.

Unit 12

Verbs

Past: It has happened.
He laughed.

Present: It is happening now.
He laughs.

Future: It will happen.
He will laugh.

2 Rewrite the sentences by changing the word in brackets to the correct tense. (The first is done for you.)

a Helen (jumping) over the box. **Helen jumped over the box.**

b The athlete (jogging) around the oval. ____________________

c Dad (make) breakfast this morning. ____________________

d The car (wait) at the lights. ____________________

3 Fill in the missing verbs on the chart.

Present tense	Past tense	Future tense
I am drawing	Yesterday I drew	Tomorrow I will ____________
I laugh	Yesterday I ____________	Tomorrow I ____________
It is snowing	Yesterday it ____________	Tomorrow it ____________
My teacher ____________	Yesterday she sang	Tomorrow she ____________

4 Below is a recount by someone who tried the hard-boiled egg trick on their class mates. Some of the past-tense verbs have been left out. Put them back in.

The hard boiled-egg trick: My recount

First, I placed the hard-boiled-egg on a chair. I didn't let anyone see. Then I sat on the egg carefully. I took the other hard-boiled egg and ____________ it to the audience. Then I ____________ to put it in my mouth. What I really ____________ was I ____________ the egg in my hand. Next I ____________ loud swallowing noises. The audience really ____________ I had ____________ the egg. While they____________ watching my face, I____________ the egg in my pocket. Suddenly I ____________ grunting and pointed to the chair. "Look!" I said. "I laid an egg and it is already ____________."

Your turn to write

Plan a magic trick to present to your class. Write the procedure for the performance. Perform your trick in front of your audience, then write an evaluation. Was your trick successful, or will you have to go back to the drawing board and alter your procedure? Remember: procedures are written in the present tense.

The clause

Clauses
There are many examples of clauses in this report.

Frogs (the subject of the clause)

have (the verb)

a life cycle (object of the clause)

Look at the first 2 sentences in Fact No. 3.
- Underline the subject
- Circle the verbs
- Highlight the objects.

Seven Facts about Frogs

← **Title**

1 Introduction
Frogs are amphibians. This means that they can go on land and in the water.

← **Classifying statement**
This is the topic of the report.

2 Did you know?
Frogs have a life cycle. Frogs begin as eggs. When they hatch they are tadpoles. When they are older they lose their tails and gain legs.

3 What frogs eat
Frogs eat insects. They eat worms, slugs, cockroaches, flies and snails. Frogs hunt at night. This way they can get their food without being caught by predators.

← **Series of facts**
The series of facts includes many present-tense action verbs and descriptive adjectives.

4 Frog eggs
Frog eggs are very interesting. They are jelly-covered. The jelly sticks the eggs together. When eggs are laid, they sink to the bottom of the pond or swamp. Eggs hatch in one or two weeks.

5 Mating
Male frogs make a lot of noise. In the mating season, male frogs croak all day and all night. Female frogs don't make much noise at all. If they do croak at all, it is very weak.

6 Where frogs live
Frogs live near ponds. They like swamps. They enjoy slow-moving water. If they are not near water, their skin gets dry and they die.

7 Enemies
The main enemies of frogs are birds, snakes and turtles. People harm frogs as well. We damage the ponds and wetlands. Frogs need these to survive.

Clauses

A **clause** is a group of words that tells us about an action and the things or people involved. Clauses consist of a subject, a verb and usually include an object.

For example,

Frogs (subject)	**eat (verb)**	**insects (object)**
Who or what is doing the action?	What is happening?	Who or what is receiving the action
The do-er	*The action*	*The done-to*

To the teacher

1 The concept of clauses is a difficult one for students at this stage. It is helpful, however, if they can identify subject, verb and object.

2 This text contains many of the language features typical of an information report. Work with the students to identify the action verbs and the range of descriptive factual adjectives.

Unit 13

Subject and verb

The **subject** is the person or thing doing the action.

1 Read the clauses below and circle the verbs. Draw a box around the subjects. (The first one is done for you.)

a Frogs are amphibians.

b Frogs eat insects.

c They like swamps.

d They eat worms, slugs, cockroaches, flies and snails.

e Frogs have a life cycle.

f Tadpoles need water.

The object

The **object** in a clause is the person or thing receiving the action of the verb.

2 Choose from the objects in the box to complete the clauses. (The first one is done for you.)

a Mary had ***a little lamb***.

b Jack and Jill fetched ______________________

c The Grand Old Duke of York has ______________________

d Simple Simon met ______________________

e Little Bo Peep lost ______________________

f Georgie Porgie kissed ______________________

g A crooked man walked ______________________

h Humpty Dumpty had ______________________

I Little Jack Horner ate ______________________

> a pie man
> a little lamb
> a Christmas pie
> a great fall
> a crooked mile
> the girls
> a pail of water
> ten thousand men
> her sheep

3 Read the sentences again in Question 2. Circle the action verb in each clause and highlight the subject.

4 Fill in the missing subjects, verbs and objects. (Look again at the report.)

Subject (do-er)	Verb	Object (done-to)
People	harm	frogs.
Frogs	______________	insects.
They	______________	their tails.
We	damage	______________ .

Your turn to write

Present your next project like the text opposite. Decide on a topic. In your first sentence define your subject. Then present a series of facts about your subject. Remember to use present-tense action verbs and many adjectives which give exact descriptions about your topic.

Adjectives

Adjectives give information about nouns or pronouns. They describe things.

1 There are many adjectives in this information report. Circle them.

Spiders – An Information Report

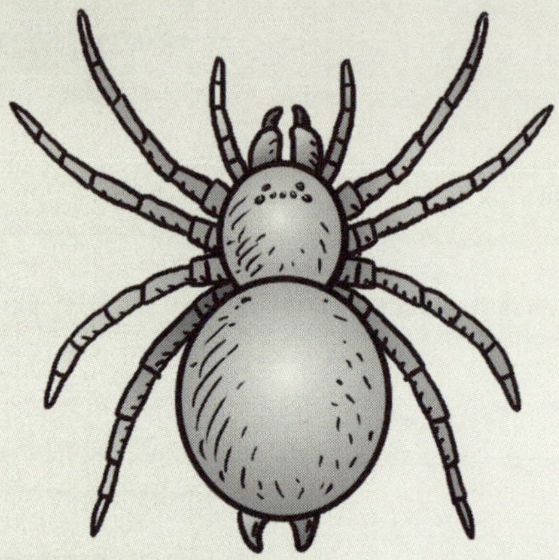

Underside view of a spider

Spiders belong to a group of animals called arachnids. With their hairy bodies and long legs, spiders provoke fear and fascination. Like an insect, a spider has jointed legs and a hard body called a carapace. Their bodies are divided into two parts separated by a slender waist and they have eight legs rather than six. Spiders have many eyes and powerful jaws that can deliver a poisonous bite.

2 Write these numbering adjectives in sentences.

a ten ______________________

b three ______________________

3 Complete the table with the missing forms of adjectives.

Word	Comparative	Superlative
great	greater	greatest
smart		
	easier	
		tidiest
	sadder	
		prettiest
small		
	longer	

Verbs

There are different kinds of verbs, such as **doing, being, saying, thinking and helping verbs**.

4 Read the short recount. Rewrite the recount, replacing the underlined verbs with more interesting verbs.

The Farm School – A Recount

Last Friday we went to the Farm School. When we got there we met the teacher. Then we fed the horses, patted the goat and held the kitten. At noon we had lunch, then we got into the bus and went home.

The Farm School – A Recount

____

____

____

____

____

5 Complete this table, using the correct verbs.

Past tense	Present tense	Future tense
He sent a letter	He is sending a letter	He will send a letter
		Jenny will cut the ribbon
They walked to school		
	Mia is having a party	
The cat jumped the fence		

The clause

A **clause** is a group of words that tells us about an action and the people involved.

6 Underline the subjects in the clauses, and draw a border around the objects. Write the verbs on the lines. (The first is done for you.)

a The spider ate the butterfly. ate

b The truck approached the intersection. ______________

c The lion caught the gazelle. ______________

d The bushfire scorched the timber shed. ______________

e The whirling tornado battered the sinking ship. ______________

Adverbs
tell us about the verb.

How to Make a Balloon-powered Rocket

Goal: Stated in the heading

Materials

Materials

a long thin balloon
masking tape
two metres of string
a plastic drinking straw
scissors

What to do

Steps: The steps are written in the order in which they should be completed.

1 Tie one end of the string to a stationary object, such as a chair.
2 Carefully thread the string through the straw.
3 Tie the other end of the string to an object two metres away. (Make sure that the string is tied firmly.)
4 Cut two pieces of masking tape.
5 Gently blow a little air into the balloon.
6 Hold the neck of the balloon tightly so the air does not escape.
7 Firmly tape the balloon to the straw.
8 Make sure the string is stretched tightly.
9 Blow a little more air into the balloon.
10 Quickly release the end of the balloon.

tells us about the verb thread (Carefully)

tells us about the verb tape (Firmly)

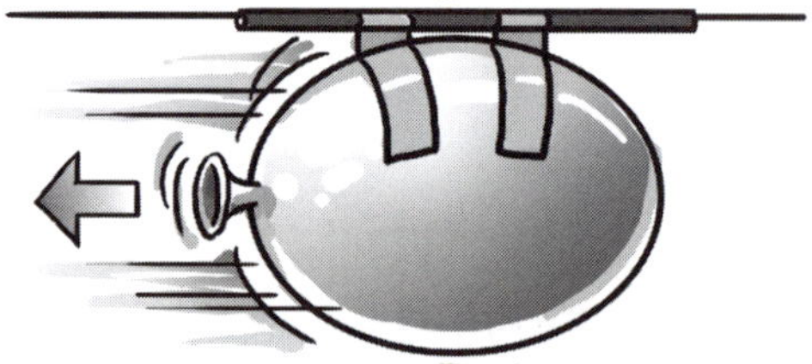

Evaluation

Evaluation

Did the balloon travel rapidly along the string? If it did, then your experiment was a success. If it did not, try again. Try using longer string and make sure the string is tight.

Adverbs

Look at the *What to do* section of the procedure. Each instruction begins with an action verb. These verbs are commands, or instructions, because they instruct us in what to do. Close to the verb is an adverb, which tells us how to do it.

For example: Firmly tape the balloon to the straw.

The adverb: tells us how to do it. The verb: tells us what to do.

1 Fill the gaps with the correct adverb from the *What to do* section.

a ________________ blow **b** ________________ release **c** ________________ thread

2 Find the adverbs which tell more about these verbs.

a is tied ________________ **b** is stretched ________________ **c** travel ________________

To the teacher

1 Talk about the function of action verbs as commands in procedures. Play some games relating to these verbs, for example, Simon says … *jump! gently scratch your left ear* … etc.
2 Note that commands often, but not always, begin the sentence. (Sometimes they are preceded by an adverb.)

Unit 15

Adverbs

Adverbs often tell us how and when.

How?	carefully, thoroughly, gently, exactly, firmly, rapidly, slowly
When?	firstly, finally, now, early, later, before, soon, after

3 Use the adverbs above to fill the gaps in the instructions.

How to make jelly

a ________________ empty one packet of jelly crystals into a jug. (You do this first.)

b ________________ add 250 mL of boiling water. (Don't burn yourself.)

c Stir ________________ until the jelly crystals dissolve. (Give it a thorough stir.)

d Add ________________ 200 mL of cold water. (Not 190 mL or 205 mL)

e ________________ pour mixture into a bowl. (Don't pour it quickly.)

f ________________ refrigerate until firm. (You do this last.)

4 The adverbs describe the actions. Think of three more adverbs to describe how the actions in the pictures could be done.

eating
greedily

____

____

____

running
rapidly

____

____

____

singing
sweetly

____

____

____

5 Change the adjectives into adverbs by adding *ly*.

careful	________	firm	________	tight	________
angry	________	noisy	________	rapid	________
quick	________	happy	________	hungry	________

Your turn to write

Design your own paper flying craft. The goal is for your craft to fly further than those designed by anyone else in your class. When you have perfected your design, write a procedure on how it could be made. See if class members can follow your directions.

Prepositions

Prepositions are usually found in front of nouns or pronouns.

preposition

The Visitor

Title

A crumbling churchyard, the sea and the moon;
The waves had gouged out grave and bone;
A man was walking, late and alone . . .

Rhyming couplets
Two-line verses with the end words rhyming

He saw a skeleton white on the ground;
A ring on a bony hand he found.

He ran home to his wife and gave her the ring.
"Oh, where did you get it?" He said not a thing.

"It's the prettiest ring in the world," she said,
As it glowed on her finger. They slipped off to bed.

At midnight they woke. In the dark outside,
"Give me my ring!" a chill voice cried.

"What was that, William? What did it say?"
"Don't worry, my dear. It'll soon go away."

"I'm coming!" A skeleton opened the door.
"Give me my ring!" It was crossing the floor.

"What was that, William? What did it say?"
"Don't worry, my dear. It'll soon go away."

"I'm touching you now. I'm climbing the bed."
The wife pulled the sheet right over her head.

It was torn from her grasp and tossed in the air:
"I'll drag you out of your bed by the hair!"

"What was that, William? What did it say?"
"Throw the ring through the window! THROW IT AWAY!"

She threw it. The skeleton leapt from the sill,
Scooped up the ring and clattered downhill,
Fainter . . . and fainter . . . Then all was still.

Ian Serraillier

Poet

They often show:

- the position of things
- the direction of things

Prepositions

A **preposition** shows the connection between a noun or pronoun and other words in a sentence. For example:
He saw the skeleton on the ground. Where was the skeleton? On the ground

1 Find the prepositions in the poem which go in front of the nouns.

________ the ground	________ the sill	________ her finger	________ the world
________ the window	________ her head	________ to bed	________ her grasp

To the teacher

Talk about the poem – it is a ballad (it tells a story). This poem features rhyming couplets. Look at the variation in the first and last verses.
Note that prepositions are often at the beginning of phrases.

Answer pages

Unit 1

1 a) aunt. **b)** holiday. **c)** mountains. **d)** house. **2 a)** night. **b)** bed. **c)** moon. **d)** trees. **3** night, holidays. **4 a)** Parts of the body: eyes, head, nose. Parts of a house: windows, roof, skylight, floor, room. Animals: possums. Plants: trees, bamboo. Furniture: bed, cupboard. **b)** Teacher. **5** possums, ball, nose, bed, mountains, night, shadows, room, head, morning, windows, cupboard. **6** Teacher. **7 a)** kindness, happiness, silliness. **b)** heroism, patriotism, sensationalism. c) tolerance, guidance, annoyance.

Unit 2

1 a) Mr Heinze. **b)** Friday 3 November. **c)** Montrose. **d)** Mrs Attard. **e)** Sow What. **2** Mt Dandenong, Victoria. **3** Teacher. **4** November, American President, Theodore (Teddy) Roosevelt, Mississippi, Clifford Berryman, Washington Post, Morris Michtom, American, Smithsonian Museum, Kermit, National Museum, American History. **5** teddy bear – Theodore (Teddy Roosevelt); sandwich – John Montague, Earl of Sandwich; bloomers – Amelia Jenks Bloomer; chauvinist – Nicholas Chauvin; diesel – Rudolf Diesel; pasteurise – Louis Pasteur; saxophone – Adolph Sax; sideburns – Ambrose Everett Burnside; biro – Lazlo Biro. **6** Teacher.

Unit 3

1 a litter of pups, a team of horses, a gaggle of geese, a brood of chickens, a herd of cows. **2** family. **3** a forest of trees, a pack of cards, a suit of clothes, a library of books, a bunch of flowers, a chest of drawers, a batch of cakes. **4** Teacher.

Unit 4

1 sunlight, sunman, sunflakes, sunball, sunbanks, sunmobile. **2** snowflakes. **3** Teacher. **4** Two words joined together: weekend, hairbrush, swagman, stingray, bathroom; Two separate words: second cousin, ground floor, space shuttle, apple tree; Two words joined by a hyphen: man-eater, red-hot, wood-shed, half-sister, three-year-old, pea-shooter. **5** Teacher.

Unit 5

1 Teacher. **2** we, us, him, them. **3** She, she, she. **4 b)** The milk is yours. **c)** The dogs are ours. **d)** The tickets are theirs. **5** Pronouns about yourself: I, me, mine; Pronouns about females: she, hers, her; Pronouns about males: him, his, he; Pronouns about others: they, theirs, yours, you, it. **6** Teacher.

Unit 6

1 whales, cheetahs, tigers, elephants, gorillas, birds (rhinoceros – singular or plural). **2** armies, cities, parties, bodies. **3** Teacher. **4 a)** foxes, lynxes, asses. **b)** ostriches, brushes, watches. **c)** donkeys, boys, toys, monkeys. **d)** shelves, calves, knives, leaves. **5 a)** tomato, hero. **b)** fly, family, injury. **6** hippos, rhinos. **7 a)** scissors. **b)** deer. **c)** moose. **d)** trout. **e)** geese. **f)** teeth. **g)** mice. **h)** trousers. **8** thieves, mousetraps – Teacher to check sentences.

Unit 7

1 Teacher. **2** blanket, car, doll, fingers, hippo, ring, pie, sun, paper, shark, jaws, cry (can be a noun or a verb), flour, arrow, baby. **3** 2 branch – branches; 5 fox – foxes; 8 radish – radishes; 1 boss – bosses; 6 party – parties; 3 city – cities; 4 donkey – donkeys; 9 thief – thieves; 12 wolf – wolves; 11 wife – wives; 7 potato – potatoes; 10 tomato – tomatoes. **4** sickness, happiness, laziness, sadness; attraction, admiration, explanation, distraction; enjoyment, appointment, encouragement, judgement. **5** truth, sadness, bravery, freedom, exhaustion, fairness, conclusion. **6** Peter Snyman, Johannesburg, South Africa, Egyptian, May. **7 a)** swarm. **b)** pack. **c)** litter. **d)** brood. **e)** fleet. **f)** library. **g)** flock. **h)** school. **i)** bunch. **j)** herd. **k) & l)** Teacher. **8** gangplank, birthday, playtime, snowball, sunset, rainstorm, stingray, airport.

Unit 8

1 best friends; some things; hardest part; big, thick dictionary; two-wheeled bike; picket fences. **2** Teacher. **3 a)** patchy. **b)** bushy. **c)** white. **d)** bald. **e)** huge. **f)** angry. **g)** tiny. **4** Teacher. **5** thoughtful, careful, helpful, wasteful; cloudy, windy, sunny, foggy; dangerous, marvellous, mountainous, adventurous.

Unit 9

1 Teacher. **2** Teacher. **3** good, **better**, best; bad, worse, **worst**; sorry, **sorrier**, **sorriest**; **brave**, braver, **bravest**; **high**, **higher**, highest; **4** disgusting, **more disgusting**, most disgusting; **wonderful**, more wonderful, **most wonderful**; beautiful, **more beautiful**, **most beautiful**. **5 a)** taller. **b)** smaller. **c)** tallest. **d)** more. **e)** most. **f)** smallest. **6** Teacher. **7 a)** smaller. **b)** worst. **c)** biggest, most. **d)** most entertaining. **e)** fastest.

Unit 10

1 skate, twist, ride. **2** ride, reel, rip, rocket, run. **3** crouch, swoop. **4** On the basketball court: leap, move, dodge, take, fly, give, drive; In the swimming pool: launch, explode, splash, blow, shake, slip, play; On the athletics track: run, sprint, look, strain, explode. **5** Teacher.

Unit 11

1 drink, feed, creep, cut, lap, called, feed, return, suck. **2** have bitten, have shown. **3** Teacher. **4 a) have** eaten, **am** going. **b) had** stopped. **c) will** be playing. **d) has** forgotten. **e) are** going. **5** racing, bitten, have changed, are chasing, punished. **6 a)** have. **b)** was. **c)** were. **d)** am. **e)** is.

Unit 12

1 Place, Sit, Take, Pretend, Puff, Show, Make, Point. **2 b)** The athlete jogged around the oval. **c)** Dad made breakfast this morning. **d)** The car waited at the lights. **3** Tomorrow I will draw. Yesterday I laughed. Tomorrow I will laugh. Yesterday it snowed. Tomorrow it will snow. My teacher is singing. Tomorrow she will sing. **4** showed, pretended, did, hid, made, thought, swallowed, were, slipped, started, cooked.

Unit 13

1 Verbs: **b)** eat. **c)** like. **d)** eat. **e)** have. **f)** need. Subjects: **b)** Frogs. **c)** They. **d)** They. **e)** Frogs. **f)** Tadpoles. **2 b)** a pail of water. **c)** ten thousand men. **d)** a pie man. **e)** her sheep. **f)** the girls. **g)** a crooked mile. **h)** a fall. **i)** a Christmas pie. **3 Action verbs**: **b)** fetched. **c)** has. **d)** met. **e)** lost. **f)** kissed. **g)** walked. **h)** had. **i)** ate. **Subject**: **b)** Jack and Jill. **c)** The Grand Old Duke of York. **d)** Simple Simon. **e)** Little Bo Peep. **f)** Georgie Porgie. **g)** A crooked man. **h)** Humpty Dumpty. **i)** Little Jack Horner. **4** Frogs eat insects. They lose their tails. We damage the ponds and wetlands.

Unit 14

1 hairy, long, jointed, hard, two, slender, eight, many, powerful, poisonous. **2** Teacher. **3** smart, **smarter, smartest; easy**, easier, **easiest**; **tidy, tidier**, tidiest; **sad**, sadder, **saddest**; **pretty, prettier**, prettiest; small, **smaller, smallest**; long, **longer, longest**. **4** Teacher. **5** Past tense: Jenny cut the ribbon; Mia had a party. Present tense: Jenny is cutting the ribbon; They are walking to school; The cat is jumping the fence. Future tense: They will walk to school; Mia will have a party; The cat will jump the fence. **6** Subjects: **b)** The truck. **c)** The lion. **d)** The bushfire. **e)** The whirling tornado. Objects: **b)** the intersection. **c)** the gazelle. **d)** the timber shed. **e)** the sinking ship. Verbs: **b)** approached. **c)** caught. **d)** scorched. **e)** battered.

Unit 15

1 a) Gently. **b)** Quickly. **c)** Carefully. **2 a)** firmly. **b)** tightly. **c)** rapidly. **3 a)** Firstly. **b)** Carefully. **c)** thoroughly. **d)** exactly. **e)** Slowly. **f)** Finally. **4** Teacher. **5** carefully, firmly, tightly, angrily, noisily, rapidly, quickly, happily, hungrily.

Unit 16

1 on the ground, **from** the sill, **on** her finger, **in** the world, **through** the window, **over** her head, **off** to bed, **from** her grasp. **2 a)** The skeleton crept over the bed. **b)** She heard the noise inside her house. **c)** The skeleton climbed down the stairs. **d)** The bell tolled before midnight. **e)** The skeleton hovered beneath the portrait. **3** on, to, under, through, onto, towards, on, through, along, onto, before.

Unit 17

1 on this subject. **2** in uniforms, beneath anyone else, against one another. **3** against **school uniforms**; from **being creative**; in **fashionable clothes.** **4** at school, on equal terms, in the morning. **5 a)** across the yard, over the rake, around the pond, into the hay stack, through the fence, under the beehive, towards the house. **b)** in time for dinner. **c)** went, walked, arrived. **d)** Teacher. **6 a)** in the morning – when. **b)** to the moon – where. **c)** with all his strength – how. **d)** with great speed – how. **e)** on the stroke of midnight – when. **f)** towards the winning post – where.

Unit 18

1 a) when, so. **b)** but. **c)** so. **d)** if. **2** Teacher. **3 b)** Toni ran fast, but Lori ran faster. **c)** The teacher was late so the class played up. **d)** Eat your dinner now or it will get cold. **e)** Exercise is important because it keeps you fit. **f)** I like spaghetti and I like baked beans.

Unit 19

1 a) On the stroke of midnight, from nowhere, with a loud roar. **b)** licking, slipping, standing. **c)** Slowly, Desperately. **d)** When, As. **e)** "Help! Help!" I yelled, but there was nobody there to listen. **2** Teacher. **3** Teacher. **4 a)** Licking. **b)** Stumbling. **c)** Feeling. **d)** Slipping. **e)** Tumbling. **5** Teacher. **6** Teacher.

Unit 20

1 Verbs: **b)** slice. **c)** fold. **d)** stand, listen. Adjectives: **b)** thinly. **c)** carefully. **d)** firstly, secondly. **2** Teacher. **3** Adverbs of manner: heavily, neatly, briskly, carefully, clearly; Adverbs of time: afterwards, later, daily, yearly; Adverbs of place: here, there, nowhere, up. **4 a)** with. **b)** towards. **c)** by. **d)** of. **e)** from. **f)** in. **g)** on. **h)** for. **i)** at. **j)** with. **5 b) with** one big bite. **c) in** an angry voice. **d) with** a loud bang. **6 b) before** her sister. **c) on** Saturday. **d) after** school. **7** Teacher.

Unit 21

1–3 Teacher counts with students. **4** Teacher. **5 a)** Watch your head! **b)** Stop thief! **c)** Go outside now! **d)** Catch the ball! **6** Teacher, e.g. Who hit you? Where did you find the kitten? Why are you yawning?

Unit 22

1 a) You could put toothpaste, toothbrushes and floss in the gift box. **b)** You should not send play money, plasticine or seeds. **c)** Wrapped hard lollies are all right, but not chocolates. **d)** Sharp items such as knives, scissors and blades should not be sent. **e)** If you think something might be good to send, check with your teacher first. **2.** Teacher. **3 a)** If possible, send these items to school, but they must be new. **b)** It is called, 'Operation Christmas Child'. **c)** You could send something to wear, such as caps, beanies, underclothes, sunglasses, polo shirts or scarves. **d)** A shoe box is not very big, so remember to choose small items. **4** Teacher.

Unit 23

1 b) Maggie Loebert's review. **c)** Albus Dumbledore's younger brother. **d)** Luna Lovegood's father. **e)** Harry's desperate quests. **2 b)** policeman's hat. **c)** lion's mane. **3 b)** the seals' beach balls. **c)** the teachers' teacups. **4 b)** the mice's cheeses. **c)** the men's hats. **5** Longer form: the antlers belonging to all the deer, the bone belonging to the dog, the flowers belonging to the women; Shorter form: the sheep's paddocks, the men's trousers.

Unit 24

1 didn't, could've, we'd, I'd, couldn't. **2** I'd – 4; We'd – 2. **3** Teacher. **4 a)** aren't, didn't, doesn't, can't, shouldn't, couldn't, won't. **b)** I'll, that's, it's, he's, she's. **5 a)** They're not allowed to play in mud because they'll get dirty. **b)** I can't come to the party because I don't have time. **c)** I'll be there, she'll be there and he's coming, too. **6** Teacher.

Unit 25

1 Highlight: "Are these homemade? They really do taste good!! We could open our own cake shop." "That's a great idea! We will call it The Red Wolf Café." **2** He opened the basket and asked, "Are these homemade?" They really do taste good!! We could open our own cake shop." **3 a)** The wolf said, "We could open a cake shop." **b)** "That's a great idea!" Little Red Riding Hood replied. **c)** "What will we call it?" asked the wolf. **d)** Red Riding Hood thought for a minute and suggested, "We'll call it Red Wolf Café." **e)** "We want to be waiters," demanded the three pigs. **f)** "I'll be the chef," cried Red Riding Hood. **g)** Grandma sighed, "I'll do the dishes." **h)** "Leave me to count the money," sniggered the wolf. **i)** Then they all shouted, "The Red Wolf Café is open for business!" **4** "Why are you late?" asked the mother. "My watch stopped," the girl replied. "Where have you been?" asked the father. "I've been looking for a dog to eat the bone," said the boy. **5** Teacher.

Unit 26

1 b) Crocodiles live in swamps. **c)** The sun was humankind's first clock. **d)** Eggs are a good form of protein. **e)** Apes are the nearest relative to humans. **f)** The skin is our largest organ. **2 b)** How long have you been at school? **c)** When do you sleep in? **d)** How do you get to school? **e)** How are you feeling? **f)** Where will we eat? **3 b)** Watch out for the traffic! **c)** Get out now! **d)** We are going! **e)** Don't write on the book! **f)** Stop crying! **4 a)** She took her umbrella, her raincoat and her hat to the football. **b)** The road was wet, muddy, slippery and dangerous. **c)** I like cheese, tomato, salami, peppers and chilli on my pizza. **5** Teacher. **6** Teacher: work with the students. Some words may need to be omitted.

Unit 27

1 a) peep, peer. **b)** scream, squawk, wail, yell. **2** forget/remember; youngest/oldest; hate/love; easy/hard; bad/good; less/more. **Challenge**: brothers and sisters – siblings. **3–5** Teacher. **6 a)** unnecessary. **b)** indigestible. **c)** incorrect. **d)** unfair. **e)** disobey. **f)** undo. **g)** incapable. **h)** invisible. **i)** disadvantage. **j)** unusual. **k)** disloyal. **l)** unkind.

Unit 28

1 a) I am ten. You can have your own car. **b)** You can go to parties and you can see anyone you like. **2** question, statement, command, exclamation, question, exclamation, command. **3 a)** I want to go swimming but it is too cold. **b)** She won the marathon because she trained really hard. **c)** I bought chicken and salad. **4 a)** Twenty-five is a good age. You are not over the hill. **b)** I am ten. I can't stay up late. **c)** You can get your bags. You can get your shoes.

Unit 29

1 Find, Wrap, Use, Decide, Fill, Stack. **2 a)** Wrap the box separately. Use colourful paper. **b)** Stack your box carefully. **3 a)** Send toys in the box. Send a letter in the shoe box. **b)** Put your letter in an envelope. **c)** You can help poor children … **d), e), f)** Teacher.

Unit 30

1 a) Baboushka, Jesus; Bethlehem, Russia. **b)** Teacher. **2** her, herself, them, themselves, they, she, I, their. **3 a)** visited, dressed, begged, followed, wanted, filled, seemed. **b)** are visited, was sitting, could wait, had fallen, could follow. **c)** Teacher. **4 a)** suddenly, unfortunately, really. **b)** Teacher. **5** freezing winter's night; cosy log cabin; huge pine-log fire; glittering star; wise men. **6 a)** Teacher **b)** Yes I will go, but I'll wait until tomorrow. **7** Teacher.

Unit 16

Prepositions

A **preposition** often tells about time and place.

Preposition word bank

above	across	along	around	among	against	after	before	behind	below	beneath
between	beside	in	into	on	onto	by	at	to	up	of
upon	down	through	off	under	over	with	within	without	near	towards

2 Change the prepositions below to give each sentence the opposite meaning.

a The skeleton crept under the bed.

____

b She heard the noise outside the house.

____

c The skeleton climbed up the stairs.

____

d The bell tolled after midnight.

____

e The skeleton hovered above the portrait.

____

3 How did Gerald wake up in time for school?

Read what happened and then write in the missing prepositions.

Use the word bank to help you to find the best prepositions. Choose a different preposition for each gap.

Gerald's patented alarm clock

I put the brick ________ the chair. I tied the string ________ the brick. I placed the candle ________ the string. The candle burned ________ the string. The iron dropped ________ the balance board. The balance board flew up high. Then the flower pot hurtled ________ the off/on switch. The switch turned ________ the fan. The fan blew ________ the funnel. The stone rolled ________ the pipe and knocked the glass. The glass tipped the water ________ my head.

So I woke up. BUT I still didn't get to school ________ the bell went.

Your turn to write

Design your own alarm clock. Write your instructions on how to use it.

Grammar focus

Adverbial phrases

Discussion structure

Adverbial phrases tell us more about the verb.

Should Uniforms Be Compulsory at My School?

← **Title**

← **Opening statement** What is the issue?

Yesterday, the parents were discussing whether there should be compulsory school uniforms. I want to tell you what I think on this subject!

← **Arguments for** *Firstly* *Secondly*

Firstly, I think kids feel good in uniforms. They feel equal with the other children. No one feels beneath anyone else. Children will not need to compete against one another.

Secondly, wearing uniforms gives kids a sense of togetherness. Kids like being a part of something. What is more, uniforms can be worn for excursions or at a sporting event.

← **Arguments against** *On the other hand*

On the other hand, some people argue strongly against school uniforms. They say that children are prevented from being creative if they all have to wear the same clothes. Some parents just like to see their children dressed in fashionable clothes.

adverbial phrase (It tells us more about the verb **dressed**) → in fashionable clothes

← **Conclusion** Restates position

After considering both sides, I feel strongly that uniforms should be worn at school. Then all of us will be on equal terms. My last reason is the most convincing of all. Just imagine, when you wake up in the morning, you will not have to think: "What am I going to wear to school today?"

Jessica, Gr. 5

Adverbial phrases

An **adverbial phrase** is a group of words which does not contain a verb. It tells us how, when, where or why about a verb. Phrases begin with prepositions.

1 **Look at the opening statement. Circle the preposition *on*. Underline the whole phrase.**

2 **Look at the second paragraph. Circle the prepositions *in*, *beneath* and *against*. Underline the phrases connected to them.**

3 **Look at the paragraph beginning "On the other hand ...". Write the phrases which begin with these prepositions:**

against ____________ ____________ from ____________ ____________ in ____________ ____________

4 **Look at the concluding paragraph. Circle the prepositions *at*, *on* and *in*. Underline the phrases connected to them.**

To the teacher

The phrase is a difficult concept for students at this level. It is probably sufficient for them to be familiar with the fact that the phrase begins with a preposition and that adverbial phrases do the work of adverbs. If you feel it is appropriate, discuss adjectival phrases. (They do the work of adjectives.)

Phrases

You can build very long sentences using adverbial phrases. Below is a retelling of the picture book *Rosie's Walk*. This is what Jenny wrote.

The Day Rosie Went for a Walk

One day Rosie went for a walk. She walked across the yard, over the rake, around the pond, into the hay stack, through the fence, under the beehive, and towards the house. She arrived in time for dinner.

by Jenny, 2F

5 Adverbial phrases tell where, when, how and why. In the retell above, there are many phrases telling *where*, and one phrase telling *when*.

a Underline the phrases telling *where* in the retell above.

b Write the phrase telling when. ______________________________

c There are only three verbs in the retell. List them.

______________ ______________ ______________

d Write your own long sentence. Use some of the prepositions from around the border.

beneath, off, into, for, across, on, below, above

The Day I Went for a Walk

One day I went for a walk. I walked

____

____

____

____

____

beside, in, through, under, towards, out, by, up, at

6 Highlight the adverbial phrases in the sentences and write whether they are telling where, when or how.

a I have to leave in the morning. ______________

b The astronaut will fly to the moon. ______________

c The weight lifter pushed with all his strength. ______________

d The yacht sailed with great speed. ______________

e The train will arrive on the stroke of midnight. ______________

f The horse galloped towards the winning post. ______________

Your turn to write

Write your own discussion on one of these topics: 'Children under twelve should not have to do homework' or 'Detention is a good thing'. Make sure you state what you think in the introduction, and include arguments for and against. In your conclusion, present a summary of your point of view.

Conjunctions

How to Keep the Brain Healthy

← Title

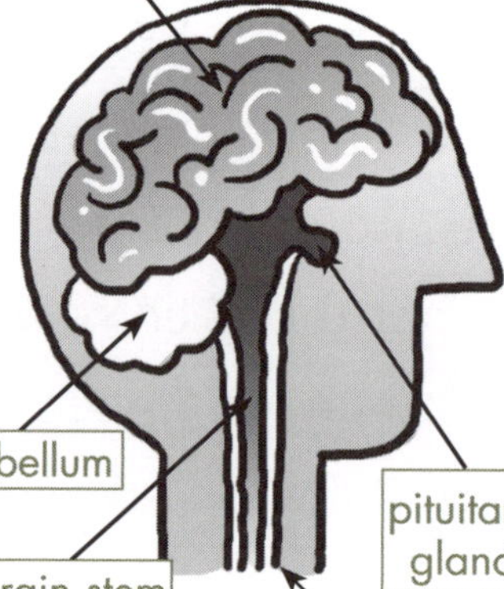

conjunction → People cannot live without a brain, so it is very important to keep it healthy.

There are a number of things that people can do to keep the brain in good condition.

← **Identifying statement** telling what is being explained

Firstly, healthy eating helps the brain.

conjunction → Secondly, exercise is important, because it helps the blood flow to the brain. As well, it is always necessary to wear a helmet when bike riding so that the head is protected.

← **Explanation sequence** *Firstly ... Secondly ... As well ...*

Smoking and too much alcohol are damaging, but the most dangerous thing of all is illegal drugs. Children, especially, should not take drugs unless they are prescribed by a doctor.

The brain starts to decline before the age of 40 – even earlier if it is not used enough. When the brain is not used, parts of it stop working. Activities like playing a musical instrument, taking up a new sport, laughing, not getting too fat, talking to friends, staying positive and not worrying too much, all help the brain.

conjunction → Last of all, it doesn't matter whether a person is old or young, the brain needs enough sleep and most important of all, if someone is feeling unhealthy, the first thing to do is to see a doctor.

← **Concluding statement**

Domenica, 5T

Conjunctions

A **conjunction** is a joining word. It joins two single words or two groups of words. The main conjunctions are:

until so but and when while after before because as if although yet unless

1 Read the text to find suitable conjunctions to complete the sentences.

a It is always necessary to wear a helmet ________ bike riding ________ that the head is protected.

b Smoking and too much alcohol are damaging, ________ the most dangerous thing of all is illegal drugs.

c People cannot live without a brain ________ it is important to keep it healthy.

d Most important of all, ________ you are feeling unhealthy, call a doctor.

To the teacher

Before doing Question 1, ask the students to highlight all the conjunctions in the explanation.

Unit 18

Conjunctions

Conjunctions help to make your writing flow.

Why I Like Jubes

I like jubes. They taste good. They are chewy. Sometimes they are a pain. They get stuck in your teeth. That's OK. I love them.

Why I Like Jubes

I like jubes because they taste good and they are chewy. Sometimes they are a pain when they get stuck in your teeth, but that's OK. I love them.

2 Explain why you like ice cream. Use conjunctions to make your writing flow.

Why I Like Ice Cream

____

____

____

____

____

3 Use the conjunctions *and*, *or*, *but* or *because* to join these sentences.

a We left early. We were tired.

We left early because we were tired.

b Toni ran fast. Lori ran faster.

____

c The teacher was late. The class played up.

____

d Eat your dinner now. It will get cold.

____

e Exercise is important. It keeps you fit.

____

f I like spaghetti. I like baked beans.

____

Your turn to write

Use the library or the Internet to research and then write a simple explanation. (Include a diagram.) Choose from "Why is the sky blue?" or "Why do stars twinkle?"

Sentences beginning with:

- adverbial phrases
- ing verbs (present tense)
- adverbs (ly words)
- conjunctions
- adjectives (describing words)
- exclaiming words.

In the Times of the Cavemen

← Title

← Orientation When? Who? Where? What?

On the stroke of midnight, I woke with a start. Nothing moved. I was in the cave and everything was quiet. Dad had been hunting all day and now he and Mum were sound asleep by the smouldering fire.

← Complication She disobeys her parents' orders

I was thirsty. Licking my lips and swallowing hard, I decided I would go down to the creek for a drink, even though my parents had said that I should not go near the creek alone. I knew they wouldn't be happy if they discovered I had gone.

← Sequence of events

Slowly, timidly, I crept out of the cave. Slipping through the undergrowth, I glimpsed the mammoths, the elks and the wild horses as they roamed in the warm night air. When I got to the creek, the water was cool and thirst-quenching.

Now it was time to return to the cave. As I turned, a dark shape appeared out of the gloom. Standing right in front of me was a baby bear. Brown, friendly eyes blinked at me. It wanted to play. I scratched its back. Frightened, it ran away and I followed it. From nowhere, a huge shape appeared. It was the mother bear. Gigantic and angry, it loomed over me. With a loud roar, it began to chase me. Desperately, I ran through the undergrowth. "Help! Help!" I yelled, but there was nobody there to listen. I looked back. The bear was gone, but I was lost. I lurched through the undergrowth. Somehow I found the cave and the huge bear was nowhere to be seen.

← Resolution

As the sun was beginning to rise, I slipped back inside. My parents were asleep and I crept into bed. That was the last time I would go wandering among the mammoths and the giants in the dead of night.

Carly, 5/6 E ← Writer

1 Look again at the text to find different ways to begin sentences.

a Highlight these adverbial phrases: *On the stroke of midnight, From nowhere, With a loud roar.*

b List three *ing* verbs. ________________ ________________ ________________

c Find two adverbs ending in *ly*. ________________ ________________

d Find and circle these conjunctions in the narrative: *When, As.*

e Write the sentence beginning with an exclamation.

____

To the teacher

The narrative was written as part of a topic on prehistoric times. The students were asked to write a creative piece that reflected what they had learnt about cave people. Focus on the sentence beginnings. Explain that, when doing their own writing, it is preferable that students don't begin all their sentences with *I, A, The, Then, We.* It is important that their choices add interest to the narrative.

2 Use the conjunctions below to begin your own sentences.

a When ______________________________

b Until ______________________________

c As ______________________________

d After ______________________________

3 Write a sentence beginning with this phrase.

Out of nowhere ______________________________

4 Choose verbs from the verb box to complete the sentences.

a ______________ my lips, I bent down to drink the water.

b ______________ through the grass, I reached the creek.

c ______________ frightened, I ran from the giant bear.

d ______________ through the forest, we escaped at last.

e ______________ down the bank, he landed with a thump.

Verb box

feeling
tumbling
slipping
licking
stumbling

5 Use the adverb to begin your sentence.

Slowly ______________________________

____

6 Choose suitable exclamations to begin these sentences.

a "______________!" cried the girl, as the bear attacked.

b "______________ ______________!" he yelled, as the mammoth charged.

c "______________!" he shouted, when the rock landed on his head.

Challenge!

On another page, use these parts of speech to begin interesting sentences of your own.

ed words – *Terrified …, Startled …, Frightened …*

Adjectives – *Brown, friendly …, Gigantic, angry …, Long, thorny …*

Adverbs

An **adverb** tells us more about the verb. It can tell how, when or where an action is done.

1 Underline the verbs and write the adverbs on the line. (The first is done for you.)

a Sing loudly to your audience. loudly

b Thinly slice the carrots when you make the soup. ______________

c Carefully fold the sheets of paper. ______________

d Firstly, stand up and secondly listen. ______________ ______________

2 Adverbs of time are used to connect one thing with another in sequence.

Imagine you are one of the school leaders and you are asked to explain what happens at school assembly. Complete the explanation.

What Happens at School Assembly – An Explanation

First, ______________________________

Then, ______________________________

Next, ______________________________

After that, ______________________________

When ______________________________

Last of all, ______________________________

3 All the words below are adverbs. Write them in their correct boxes.

heavily here afterwards neatly
up there briskly nowhere
clearly later daily carefully yearly

Adverbs of manner (how?)	Adverbs of time (when?)	Adverbs of place (where?)

Prepositions

A **preposition** is a small word which connects one word to another in a sentence.

from in of with by at for on towards with

4 Choose one of the prepositions above to complete the sentences.

- **a** Please come __________ me.
- **b** He kicked the ball __________ the goal.
- **c** I will drop __________ to see you.
- **d** What is the price __________ the TV?
- **e** The present is __________ John.
- **f** I put your name __________ the book.
- **g** I'm glad you're __________ time.
- **h** I will pay __________ the ice creams.
- **i** The teacher arrived __________ school.
- **j** He greeted her __________ a big hug.

Adverbial phrases

A **phrase** is a group of words without a verb. An adverbial phrase tells us how, when, where about the verbs.

5 Write the phrase which tells *how* in each sentence. Circle the preposition.

- **a** He drew the picture with great care. **with great care**
- **b** He finished the pie with one big bite. ____________________
- **c** She yelled at John in an angry voice. ____________________
- **d** The fireworks began with a loud bang. ____________________

6 Write the phrase which tells *when* in each sentence. Circle the preposition.

- **a** School starts after 9 a.m. **after 9 a.m.**
- **b** She arrived before her sister. ____________________
- **c** We play the Tigers on Saturday. ____________________
- **d** Sports practice will be held after school. ____________________

7 Finish the sentences by completing the phrases telling *where*.

- **a** The thief crept through **the house**.
- **b** She put her slippers under ________________
- **c** He put the wallet in ________________
- **d** She threw the basketball into ________________
- **e** The frightened fox jumped over ________________

Grammar focus

. Full stop

? Question mark

! Exclamation mark

Questions

begin with a capital letter and end with a question mark.

Statements

begin with a capital letter and end with a full stop.

Exclamations

begin with a capital letter and end with an exclamation mark.

Stop Pentrose Quarry Expansion

- **Do we want dust?**

  It blows off gigantic stock piles.

  It settles on houses.

  It hurtles into the air with every explosion.
- **Do we want noise?**

  The trucks roar.

  The explosions rattle windows, dishes and light fittings.

  People are startled.
- **Do we want fumes?**

  They escape from the asphalt.
- **Do we want to lose vegetation?**
- **Do we want to ruin Bungalow creek?**

We say "NO!"

Protest now!

Stop them gouging into our land!

Write letters!

Give out leaflets!

DON'T let this outrage happen!

Exposition structure

Statement of position

Catchy slogan

Graphics

Series of arguments

Repetition

Do we want…?

Supporting evidence in the form of statements

Call for action in the form of exclamations

Reinforcement of position taken

1 **Highlight the questions. How many questions?** ☐

2 **Underline the statements. How many statements?** ☐

3 **Circle the exclamations. How many exclamations?** ☐

To the teacher

1 Talk about the different types of expository texts. Arguments are used to put forward one point of view. Discussions are when different points of view are presented. Advertisements are used to promote a product or a point of view.

2 In the poster above, questions, exclamations, statements and graphics are used to promote a point of view.

Unit 21

Statements

A **statement** is a sentence which tells us something, for example, *You should obey the school rules.*

School Rules

1 Be polite to visitors.
2 Walk in corridors and path ways.
3 Always wear your school uniform.
4 Keep your hands and feet to yourselves.
5 Get help from the yard duty teacher.

4 What are the rules for good behaviour in your classroom?

State four class rules.

Grade 5A – Class Rules

i ______________________________

ii ______________________________

iii ______________________________

iv ______________________________

!

An **exclamation** is a sentence that shows strong feelings, such as joy, anger or fright, for example, *Quarries are bad!*

5 Rewrite the exclamations, using the correct punctuation.

a watch your head ______________________________

b stop thief ______________________________

c go outside now ______________________________

d catch the ball ______________________________

?

A **question** is a sentence that asks a question, for example, *Do we want dust?*

6 The cartoon characters below have given the answers. What were the questions? Write them in the empty speech bubbles. (Don't forget the question marks.)

Your turn to write

Choose an issue which is of particular importance to you and your school, such as: more play space, rubbish-free school, saving water, traffic pollution. Design a poster to persuade people to change. Include on your poster: graphics, various forms of print, pictures, important questions and strong exclamations.

The Christmas Shoe Box – A Letter to Parents

Commas can be used:

- after a greeting in a letter
- to separate spoken words from the rest of a sentence
- to separate different parts of a sentence
- to mark a pause in a sentence
- to divide items in a sentence (in a list there is usually no comma after the second last item if it is followed by *and*)
- in the concluding part of a letter.

(An informal letter)

1 October 2007

Dear Parents,

I am writing to ask you to help in a special project that our class is conducting this year. It is called 'Operation Christmas child'.

Have you ever asked yourself, "How can I help a child who has been hurt in a war, or a natural disaster, or is in extreme poverty?" This is your chance to help. Each grade in our school will collect a shoe box of small Christmas gifts for a boy or girl living in extreme poverty. By doing this we can bring a little joy and hope to another child, even though that child may be suffering.

It will provide an opportunity for your child to see that Christmas is a time for giving, not just receiving.

Gifts which can be used to fill the box include toys such as dolls, soft toys, trucks, cars, jigsaws, building blocks, mouth organs, T-shirts, socks, sandals, bangles and necklaces.

If possible, send these items to school, but they must be new. Second-hand items are not suitable. Please bear in mind that to fit in a shoe box, the items must be small.

After the donations have been collected, the children will be decorating the boxes before packing them, ready to send overseas. The last day for donations is Wednesday 26 October.

Many thanks,

Mrs Loebert, Grade 5L

Date

Greeting

Information in paragraphs To indicate purpose

Closing greeting

Name of writer

Commas

Commas are used to make a sentence easier to understand. A comma indicates that you should take a shorter pause than a full stop.

1 Put commas in the correct places.

- **a** You could put toothpaste toothbrushes and floss in the gift box.
- **b** You should not send play money plasticine or seeds.
- **c** Wrapped hard lollies are all right but not chocolates.
- **d** Sharp items such as knives scissors and blades should not be sent.
- **e** If you think something might be good to send check with your teacher first.

To the teacher

Transactional texts are used for interaction between two or more people. (See opposite for a reply to this letter.) This letter asks for parental help in an activity conducted by the grade. Note this is a wonderful pre-Christmas activity. See Unit 29 for a procedure (instructional) on how the students can decorate and prepare their Christmas shoe boxes.

A letter in reply

2 This letter on the right was from a parent in response to the letter sent home by the teacher. The writer left out all the commas. Follow the instructions to put them in.

Write commas:

- **a** after the greeting
- **b** after the pause in the sentence
- **c** before the spoken words
- **d** between the words in the list of items to be sent
- **e** after the pauses in the two sentences in this paragraph
- **f** after the final greeting.

5 October 2007

Dear Mrs Loebert

Thank you so much for your letter. I think "Operation Christmas Child" is a wonderful idea.

I will participate in the program even though we do not have much spare cash at the moment.

I have a few questions. First, my daughter Claire asked me "Can we send educational supplies or hygiene items?" I thought such things as felt pens colouring books puzzle books crayons erasers and stickers would be good. Also personal items such as combs hairbrushes hairclips scrunchies face washers might be helpful.

As well I was wondering how the shoe boxes get to the children. Do you organise this or does someone else do it?

Thanks again for inviting us to join in such a terrific idea.

Yours faithfully

Jenny Thompson

3 Write the commas where they belong.

- **a** If possible send these items to school but they must be new.
- **b** It is called 'Operation Christmas Child'.
- **c** You could send something to wear such as caps beanies underclothes sunglasses polo shirts or scarves.
- **d** A shoe box is not very big so remember to choose small items.

4 What other items might be included in the Christmas boxes? List things that have not already been mentioned.

The Christmas Box

Items which could be sent to the children are:

____

____

____

____

Your turn to write

Make your own Christmas card or write a Christmas letter to include in your Christmas shoe box. You will be sending a special Christmas message from Australia, and wishing the person happiness for the New Year. Put it in an envelope and place it in the box.

The apostrophe of possession

Apostrophe of possession

Possession means ownership.

The 's after a word shows that something is owned by someone.

e.g. Harry's best friends

Whose best friends are they?

Answer: Harry's

Look again at the review. Highlight all the words ending with an apostrophe 's.

BOOK REVIEW: J K Rowling's *Harry Potter and the Deathly Hallows*

Opening statement Gives background information

The Harry Potter stories by J K Rowling have broken all the records and *Harry Potter and the Deathly Hallows* is the author's seventh and last book in the series.

Summary Describes key features such as characters, plot and setting

Characters: The main character, of course, is Harry Potter. Harry's best friends, Ron and Hermione, are also central to the story. As well, there are all the characters from the previous books, including everyone from the Order of the Phoenix, Voldemort and Voldemort's creepy followers, the Death Eaters. Also included are two new characters, Albus Dumbledore's younger brother, Aberforth Dumbledore, and Luna Lovegood's father, Xenophilius.

Plot: The story is about Harry's desperate quest to find Voldemort. He knows that he will have to face Voldemort in a final battle to the death, because neither can live while the other survives. The seventh book is like a rollercoaster ride. There are lots of twists and turns and some of the characters you love die. Even though it is filled with surprises (lots of them sad), it all ends well for Harry, Ron and Hermione.

Setting: Unlike the rest of the Harry Potter books that are mostly set in Hogwarts, in the seventh book, Harry, Hermione and Ron don't go back to the school's ancient classrooms, but instead spend most of the time roaming the country's hills and valleys, facing danger wherever they go. They return to Hogwarts at the very end for the last battle between good and evil.

Rating:

★★★★½

I would have given it five out of five except one of my favourite characters dies.

Judgement and personal response

Opinion: The book is really good. It is exciting and there are heaps of twists. It was better than I expected and I would recommend it to anyone!

Maggie L. 6M

Apostrophe of possession

The **apostrophe** is placed after a word to show that something or someone belongs to it.

1 **Rewrite the following phrases using an apostrophe to show ownership.**

a the book of J K Rowling. **J K Rowling's book**

b the review of Maggie Loebert ____________________

c the younger brother of Albus Dumbledore ____________________

d the father of Luna Lovegood ____________________

e the desperate quests of Harry ____________________

To the teacher

The apostrophe 's often causes confusion. After the students have completed the activities on this page, relating to singular nouns, discuss what happens for plural nouns. (See opposite.)

Unit 23

Apostrophes

Rules for using an apostrophe to show ownership:

If there is just one owner, we add 's.

the boy's cap (the hat belonging to the boy)

If there is more than one owner, we add ' to the plural

the girls' bags (the bags belonging to the girls)

If the plural does not end in s we add 's.

the children's books (the books belonging to the children)

Rewrite the sentences using apostrophes to show possession.

2 For a singular noun, add *'s*.
The first is done for you.

a The ruler belongs to Jenny. ***Jenny's ruler***

b The hat belongs to the policeman. ____________________

c The mane belongs to the lion. ____________________

3 For plural nouns ending in *s*, add *'*.

a The kennels belonging to the dogs. ***The dogs' kennels***

b The beach balls belonging to the seals ____________________

c The teacups belonging to the teachers ____________________

4 For plural nouns not ending in *s*, add *'s*.

a The toys belonging to the children ***The children's toys***

b The cheeses belonging to the mice ____________________

c The hats belonging to the men ____________________

5 Complete this chart.

Longer form	Shorter form
the basketballs belonging to the schools	***the schools' basketballs***
the paddocks belonging to the sheep	
the trousers belonging to the men	
	the deer's antlers
	the dog's bone
	the women's flowers

Your turn to write

Select a book which you have really enjoyed. Write a review based on the model opposite. Write your review so that the reader will be encouraged to borrow or buy the book.

The apostrophe of contraction

Apostrophe of contraction
Contraction means *shorten*.

Writing task

Describe or draw your secret hiding place – real or make-believe.

Secret Club House

didn't is a contraction of did not (The o in not has been left out.)

If I had a secret club house, it would only be big enough for me and a couple of friends. Anyone who didn't know the password would not get in. I'd have a hard tongue twister like SIX SICK SILLY SOCKS, SWAM SLOWLY, SLOWLY, SPLASHING SILLILY IN SLIMY WATER – twice. You couldn't get in until you said it the right way.

Introduction Tells readers what is being described

I'd have a small coffee table, a square of carpet and lots of cushions instead of chairs. I'd cover the walls with pictures we'd made in the club house. I'd also have a small cupboard. We'd make secret plans, and talk in code.

Description of features

We would meet secretly, so that no one would know where it was. I think it would be heaps of fun to own a secret club house.

Concluding comment

Apostrophe of contraction

An **apostrophe of contraction** is used to show that letters have been left out and a word has been shortened. For example, *I'm* is the contraction of *I am*. *Should've* is the contraction of *Should have*.

Check your answers on the Contraction Table on the next page.

1 Write the contractions.

did not = ________________ could have = ________________

we would = ________________ I would = ________________

could not = ________________

2 The contractions *I'd* and *we'd* are used several times in the text above. Highlight these contractions. Count how often they are used.

I'd ☐ We'd ☐

3 Use the contraction in a sentence.

doesn't ____

____

To the teacher

Compare the use of the apostrophe in this unit with that in Unit 23 (apostrophes of possession). It is important to emphasise that the only time an apostrophe of contraction is used is when a word is shortened.

Contractions table

	Contraction		Contraction		Contraction
I will	I'll	does not	doesn't	should not	shouldn't
I am	I'm	can not	can't	could not	couldn't
are not	aren't	he is	he's	will not	wont
did not	didn't	she is	she's	would not	wouldn't
that is	that's	we are	we're	there is	there's
it is	it's	they are	they're	I have	I've

4 Use the table to write the following contractions.

a Words where the letter *o* has been left out (There are 7.)

____

b Words where the letter *i* has been left out (There are 5.)

____

5 Rewrite the sentences. Change the underlined words to contractions.

a <u>They are</u> not allowed to play in mud because <u>they will</u> get dirty.

____

b I <u>cannot</u> come to the party because I <u>do not</u> have time.

____

c <u>I will</u> be there, <u>she will</u> be there and <u>he is</u> coming, too.

____

6 Complete the crossword by writing the full words for the contractions.

Across		Down	
2	she's	1	can't
4	I'm	3	he's
7	don't	5	wasn't
8	it's	6	doesn't
11	aren't	9	that's
12	what's	10	let's

Your turn to write

Write a description. Choose from these titles: *My Secret Place*; *My Special Place*; *My Quiet Place*. In your description try to include at least eight of the contractions from the table above, including *it's* (it is); *can't* (cannot); *we'll* (we will) and *that's* (that is). The description should include an introduction, saying what is being described, and a conclusion saying why you especially like that particular place. (Note: Read some descriptions in books before you begin.)

Direct speech

The Red Wolf Café

← Title

I am sure everyone knows the story of Little Red Riding Hood, but this one ends a little differently.

One miserable rainy day, Little Red Riding Hood made her way to Grandma's house.

← **Orientation** Who? When? Where?

When she got there, she noticed the wolf in bed, so she gave him the basket of cakes.

← **Complication**

He opened the basket and asked, "Are these homemade? They really do taste good!! We could open our own cake shop."

" " Quotation marks are used to show what is spoken.

← **Sequence of events** Notice the use of dialogue. Each time a character talks, it is set out on a new line.

Little Red Riding Hood said, "That's a great idea! We will call it The Red Wolf Café," and they did.

The café was a hit. People came from everywhere. It was one busy place.

The three little pigs were waiters and Little Red Riding Hood was the chef. Grandma washed the dishes, while the wolf just counted the money, rather than eating Grandma.

So they all lived happily ever after, even the big bad wolf, who turned out to be not so bad after all.

← **Resolution**

Retold by Chloe, 5K

Direct speech

When we write the actual words spoken, it is called direct speech. For example,

"I'm going to visit Grandma," said Red Riding Hood.

(quotation marks; capital letter; comma inside speech marks; full stop)

1 Highlight the words actually spoken in the text.

2 Rewrite the sentences below, putting in all the punctuation.

he opened the basket and asked are these homemade they really do taste good we could open a cake shop

____

____

To the teacher

Discuss the role that dialogue plays in narrative. To explore how direct speech works, choose another fairy tale, such as 'The Three Little Pigs'. With the class, transform sections of the narrative into direct speech. Ask the students to rewrite a fairy tale. Ask them to include direct speech.

3 Place the quotation marks around the actual words spoken in the sentences below.

a The wolf said, We could open a cake shop.

b That's a great idea! Little Red Riding Hood replied.

c What will we call it? asked the wolf.

d Red Riding Hood thought for a minute and suggested, We'll call it Red Wolf Café.

e We want to be waiters, demanded the three pigs.

f I'll be the chef, cried Red Riding Hood.

g Grandma sighed, I'll do the dishes.

h Leave me to count the money, sniggered the wolf.

i Then they all shouted, The Red Wolf Cafe is open for business!

4 Change the words in the speech bubbles into written speech. Write on the lines below. (Don't forget the quotation marks.)

____

____

____

____

5 Complete these sentences using direct speech. (Put in the quotation marks.)

a The big bad wolf shouted, ___________________________

b When the giant saw Jack he growled, ___________________________

c Who's that sleeping ___________________________

d The ugly sister snarled ___________________________

e Mirror, Mirror ___________________________

f What big teeth ___________________________

Your turn to write

Hold a reader's theatre. Choose a narrative with lots of dialogue. Write a script in which the speech of each character is highlighted. Students in your group should read the script with great flourish and expression.

Revision

Statements

Statements begin with a capital letter and end with a full stop. They tell us something.

1 Rewrite these statements using the correct punctuation.

a every living thing needs water *Every living thing needs water.* ____

b crocodiles live in swamps ____

c the sun was humankinds first clock ____

d eggs are a good form of protein ____

e apes are the nearest relative to humans ____

f the skin is our largest organ ____

Questions

Questions begin with a capital letter and end with a question mark. A question is a sentence which asks something.

2 Write your own questions for these answers.

a My favourite fruit is apple. *What is your favourite fruit?* ____

b I have been at school for six years. ____

c We sleep in on Sundays. ____

d I ride my bike to school. ____

e I am feeling very well. ____

f We will eat at the café. ____

Exclamations

Exclamations begin with a capital letter and end with an exclamation mark. An exclamation shows strong feelings, like joy or anger.

3 Rewrite these questions as exclamations.

a Will that hurt? *That will hurt!* ____

b Will you watch out for the traffic? ____

c Will you get out now? ____

d Can we go? ____

e Must you write on the book? ____

f Are you going to stop crying? ____

Unit 26

Commas

A **comma** is a punctuation mark which is used to make a sentence easier to understand.
A comma shows that you should take a shorter pause than a full stop.

4 Write the commas in the correct places.

a She took her umbrella her raincoat and her hat to the football.

b The road was wet muddy slippery and dangerous.

c I like cheese tomato salami peppers and chilli on my pizza.

5 Complete these sentences.

a After you left, ______________________________

b No, ______________________________

c If you climb that tree, ______________________________

6 Nellie Patch never stops talking. When she meets some aliens who have invaded the township of Wallabah, her voice goes into overdrive – all the words are jammed together. Make some sense of Nellie Patch's words by writing in the correct punctuation in the extract below.

You will need to add:

- capital letters
- full stops
- commas
- exclamation marks
- question marks.

"Why hello," she said enthusiastically. "What smart green scuba diving suits you have on did you get them mail order from the city what a shame you went to all that trouble because there's nowhere round here you can go scuba diving but you could come to the picnic instead if you like you certainly are both very tall aren't you my Uncle David's a hundred and ninety centimetres in his socks but even he's not as tall as you do you want to come home and meet my Uncle David he's away he coaches this basketball team but you could call in tomorrow my address is number four Lambert Crescent the house with all the soundproofing covers over the windows that's so the neighbours won't complain mum says only they still do my it's nice to see some new faces around Wallabah we haven't had any new faces for ages not many new people come here to live and isn't it funny a lot of people seem to be moving away too now I come to think of it and I don't know why because Wallabah is a nice little town."

Klein, *How Nellie Patch Saved the Little Town of Wallabah*

7 When you have finished putting in all the punctuation, read it aloud to a friend to see if it makes sense.

Grammar focus

Synonyms and antonyms

Discussion structure

Antonyms

These are antonyms because they are opposite in meaning.

Synonyms

These words have a similar meaning.

ad good bad good bad good bad good bad good bad good bad good ba

Good and Bad Things about Having Brothers and Sisters

Title

You asked me about the good and bad things about having brothers and sisters, so here is my opinion.

Opening statement

First, I'll tell you about the bad things, but you must remember, I'm the eldest, so I'm biased.

Arguments for — Text connectives such as *First …* *As well …* *On the other hand …* *Last …* form links throughout the text

Little brothers and sisters say: "Read a story," right in the middle of your homework or a good book. They jump on your bed just as you're about to get into it. They scream and shout and wail, "Mum, Kylie won't let me play!" Little brothers pull your hair "by mistake" on long, hot car journeys. Little sisters poke and peer and peep and pry and play with your prized jewellery box.

As well as all this, they find new ways to ruin your precious items. Just imagine coming home after a hard day at school to find your brand new packet of felt pens all battered, half-lost and mostly blunt.

Last of all and worst of all, are the yells and squawks that come from exactly the same wall which is nearest to the room where you are doing your homework.

Arguments against

On the other hand, there are some good things about siblings. Being the eldest, there is no one to boss you around, while at the same time you can boss whichever one you like. Apart from that, you get lots more presents on birthdays and Christmas. Likewise, you can send them on small boring errands. Finally, it's good to have someone to share the walk to school.

Conclusion

So you can see, even though I love them all, having brothers and sisters can be a pain in the neck at times.

Kylie, Grade 5b

Synonym Antonym

A **synonym** is a word with a similar meaning to another word.
An **antonym** is a word with an opposite meaning to another word.

1 Find synonyms for these words.

a stare ____________ ____________

b shout ____________ ____________ ____________ ____________

2 Find antonyms for these words.

forget ____________ youngest ____________

hate ____________ easy ____________

bad ____________ less ____________

Challenge!

Find a synonym for brothers and sisters. ____________

To the teacher

One way that links are set up within a text is through synonyms and antonyms. A further effective means of creating cohesion in a text is through text connectives. These words provide the reader with signposts indicating how the text is developing. For example, the text is given sequence through the use of *First* ... and *Last of all* ..., and the words *As well* ... and lead the reader to expect additional information.

Unit 27

Synonyms

Synonyms can be used to create more powerful words in your writing, for example, instead of *hit* you could use the word *bash*.

3 The synonyms for *hit* are in the speech bubble. Add synonyms for the other words in the speech bubbles.

4 A good discussion needs powerful words. Rewrite the sentences using two powerful words to give a better description. (The first is done for you.)

a She hit the robber. *She belted and clobbered the robber.*

b It was a bad apple. ____________________

c Joanne is a good singer. ____________________

d The teacher yelled at him. ____________________

e The movie was bad. ____________________

5 Use a dictionary or a thesaurus. Write powerful synonyms for these words.

a treasure ____________________

b worry ____________________

c quiet ____________________

d empty ____________________

e sorry ____________________

f nice ____________________

Antonyms

You can make your discussions more powerful and interesting by using prefixes to make the opposites of words, for example, "Little brothers can be so selfish, but I am unselfish."

6 Add the prefixes *un-*, *in-* or *dis-* to these words to make antonyms.

a ______necessary	**b** ______digestible	**c** ______correct	**d** ______fair
e ______obey	**f** ______do	**g** ______capable	**h** ______visible
i ______advantage	**j** ______usual	**k** ______loyal	**l** ______kind

Your turn to write

Write a discussion about a topic which is important at your school at the moment. Remember to present both sides. While you are writing, have a thesaurus by your side so that you can choose the best words to make your discussion powerful.

If You Had the Choice, What Is the Best Age to Be?

Simple sentence
Just one clause, which makes sense on its own

Compound sentence
More than one independent clause, joined by the conjunction **because**

This a difficult question. Twenty-five is a good age. ← **Statement of position**

I am ten. I'm not a teenager yet, so it's hard to be sure. I've got an older brother, so I know a bit about what it's like to be twenty-five. You can go to parties and you can see anyone you like. You can have your own car. You can go to the movies, but you don't have to be home before midnight. You are free, because you are an adult. ← **Argument and evidence to support**

Twenty-five is a good age because you are not over the hill, but you are through the worst perils of growing up. Best of all, you're not young enough to be made to dress up in frills and bows and have everyone say, "Oh. Isn't she cute?" I HATE that!

So all in all, I think being round about twenty-five is best. ← **Concluding statement**

Sentences

A **simple sentence** has one idea in it.

For example, *Twenty five is a good age.*

(*Twenty-five* is the subject and *is a good age* is the predicate.)

A **compound sentence** has at least two ideas in it which are independent and could have been two separate sentences. For example, *You are free because you are an adult.*

The two sentences could be *You are free* and *You are an adult.* They are joined by the conjunction *because*.

1 Look at the second paragraph in the text.

a Find two simple sentences beginning with the words below.

I ______________________________

You ______________________________

b Write one compound sentence which contains the conjunction below.

and ______________________________

____

To the teacher

Look back to Unit 13 where clauses are discussed. A clause is a group of words that has a subject (something that the clause is about) and a predicate (which always includes a verb).

Sentences

A simple sentence expresses just one complete thought.
Sentences can be statements, commands, questions, exclamations.

- **statements:** *I am ten.*
- **commands:** *You must get home before midnight.*
- **questions:** *What is the best age?*
- **exclamations:** *I HATE that!*

2 Identify the simple sentences below by writing *statement*, *command*, *question* or *exclamation* in the box.

Simple sentences	Type
When is it lunch time?	
Twenty-five is a very good age.	
Stand up now.	
I love liquorice!	
May I go to the movies?	
You keep quiet!	
Kick the goal.	

3 Use the conjunctions *and*, *but* or *because* to join the simple sentences to make compound sentences.

a I want to go swimming. It is too cold.

____

b She won the marathon. She trained really hard.

____

c I bought chicken. I bought salad.

____

4 Split the compound sentences into two simple sentences. Write them. Omit the conjunctions.

a Twenty-five is a good age because you are not over the hill.

____

b I am ten, but I can't stay up late.

____

c You can get your bags and you can get your shoes.

____

Your turn to write

Write an exposition on the topic: "Should children go to school?" State your opinion first, then work out the arguments in support of your case. Don't forget to write a convincing concluding statement.

Command sentences are often used in procedures.

How to Make a Christmas Shoe Box

Goal

The shoe box is to be decorated, filled with tiny presents and sent to a child in poverty living overseas.

Goal — What you aim to do

Materials

A shoe box measuring 13–18 cm deep × 28–30 cm wide × 11–13 cm high

Colourful paper

Materials — What you need

Steps

They usually begin with an action verb.

1. Find an empty shoe box.
2. Wrap the lid and box separately. Use colourful paper.
3. Decide if the box is for a boy or girl.
4. Fill the box with gifts (small toys, games, pencils, clothes, bangles, necklaces).
5. Stack your box carefully.

The boxes can be collected and arrangements can be made to send them overseas.

Steps — Written in the order needed to complete your goal

Commands

A **command** is a kind of sentence. It is often used to instruct or tell someone what to do. (Commands often begin with an action verb.)

Read the Steps section of the procedure and do the following.

1 There are six action verbs. List them.

______ ______ ______ ______ ______ ______

2 Write the answers to these questions as commands.

a How should the box be wrapped?

____

b How should the boxes be stacked?

____

To the teacher

This is a powerful activity for the children. (See Unit 22 for the related unit about the Christmas Box. In that unit a transactional text model was presented in the form of a letter to parents, inviting their participation in the shoe box present.) For details about where to send the boxes, contact <samaritanspurse.org.au>.

Sentences

What kind of sentence is it?

- Is it a **command**? *Find a shoe box.* (Begins with an action verb)
- Is it a **question**? *Can you help?* (Ends with a question mark)
- Is it an **exclamation**? *Be generous!* (Ends with an exclamation mark)
- Is it a **statement**? *You can help poor children.*

3 The poster below uses commands, questions, exclamations and statements to persuade people to make a Christmas shoe box. Read it and then complete the activities.

a Write two commands beginning with the verb *send*.

____________________ ____________________

b One command is in brackets. Write it. ____________________

c Write a statement beginning with: You ____________________

d Add one command of your own to the poster.

e Circle all the commands in the poster. Underline the action verbs.

f Highlight the questions. Colour the exclamations.

Your turn to write

Design your own poster to advertise an important event coming up soon at your school. As a special challenge, your poster must contain four commands and at least two questions, two exclamations and two statements.

Narrative structure

Baboushka – a Christmas Story

← **Title**

← **Orientation** Where? Why? Who? When?

In Russia, Santa Claus does not bring presents. The children are visited by an old woman called Baboushka, the Russian word for 'grandmother'.

← **Complication**

One freezing winter's night, Baboushka was sitting in her cosy log cabin in the woods, warming herself in front of a huge, pine-log fire.

Suddenly there was a knock on the door. Standing outside were three visitors, dressed in exotic clothes. Baboushka invited them inside to warm themselves, and they begged her to join them as they followed the glittering star which was to lead them to the Baby Jesus in the stable at Bethlehem.

← **Sequence of events**

Baboushka really wanted to go, but it was bitterly cold and she thought to herself, "Yes, I will go, but I'll wait until tomorrow. Perhaps the weather will change."

She put another log on the fire, and the wise men could wait no longer. They had to set off without her.

The next day Baboushka was filled with remorse, and she set off to follow the wise men. Unfortunately, snow had fallen and she couldn't find their tracks. There was no way that she could follow them! The star, of course, had gone.

She ran this way and that, begging people to tell her where to find the Holy Child.

No one seemed to know.

← **Resolution**

She roamed the countryside, leaving presents for the children, always hoping in her heart to meet Jesus.

A Russian legend

The narrative contains most of the important parts of speech. Read it again and do the activities.

Nouns

Nouns name people, places or things.

Baboushka (noun)
donkey (noun)

1 a Write the names of two people. ______________ ______________

Write the names of two places. ______________ ______________

b Write the plural of this noun in a sentence.

child ____

Pronouns

Pronouns are used in place of nouns.

they (pronoun)
them (pronoun)

2 There are several different pronouns in the text. Draw a box around them.

To the teacher

The narrative is the ideal vehicle to revise the different parts of speech, as it normally incorporates the following grammatical features: noun groups (nouns, pronouns, adjectives); verb groups (past-tense verbs); adverbial groups (adverbs and phrases – about when, where); text connectives and conjunctions.

Unit 30

Verbs

Verbs are doing, being or having words.

sat (verb)

walked (verb)

3 **a** Find seven past-tense verbs ending in *ed*.

____

b Helper verbs are: *is, am, are, was, were, been, has, had, will, would, could, should, might*. Find the helper verbs which go in front of these verbs.

__________ visited __________ sitting __________ wait __________ fallen __________ follow

Adverbs

Adverbs often tell how, when, where or how much.

sit quietly (adverb)

trudge slowly (adverb)

4 **a** Find three adverbs ending in *ly*. __________ __________ __________

b Write sentences beginning with these adverbs.

Suddenly ______________________________

Slowly ______________________________

Adjectives

Adjectives are describing words.

old woman (adjective)

small donkey (adjective)

5 **Find adjectives to describe these nouns.**

__________ __________ night __________ __________ cabin

__________ __________ fire __________ star __________ men

Conjunctions

Conjunctions are joining words.

The donkey is old, but the woman is older.

6 **a** Circle the conjunctions *as, and, but* in the text.

b Use a conjunction to make these into one longer sentence.

Yes I will go. I'll wait until tomorrow.

____

Prepositions

Prepositions often show the position or direction of things.

The woman is sitting on the donkey.

The donkey is walking behind the man.

7 **a** These prepositions are in the text. Highlight them.

by for in of on inside off

b Write three of the prepositions above in *one* sentence of your own.

____

Self-assessment

Recount – A recount retells a series of events in the order that they happened.

	Yes	No
Purpose: Does it tell about past events?	☐	☐
Structure: When I write a recount, I include:		
• an orientation telling who, where, when	☐	☐
• a series of events in order	☐	☐
• a personal comment.	☐	☐
Forms: I can write:		
• a diary extract	☐	☐
• a personal letter	☐	☐
• a postcard	☐	☐
• an email.	☐	☐

	Yes	No
Grammar: I have used:		
• common nouns, e.g. shop, tin, school	☐	☐
• proper nouns, e.g. Tom, Sydney	☐	☐
• personal pronouns, e.g. she, we	☐	☐
• past-tense action verbs, e.g. jumped, walked	☐	☐
• time and sequence words, e.g. first, next	☐	☐
• adverbial phrases, e.g. with a hammer, in the car.	☐	☐
TOTAL	☐	☐

Information report – An information report gives accurate and factual information about a class of living and non-living things.

	Yes	No
Purpose: Does it give information about a class of living or non-living things?	☐	☐
Structure: When I write an information report, I include:		
• classifying statement	☐	☐
• series of facts.	☐	☐
Forms: I can write:		
• a science report	☐	☐
• an information chart.	☐	☐

	Yes	No
Grammar: I have used:		
• common nouns	☐	☐
• technical nouns, e.g. mammal, oxygen	☐	☐
• present-tense verbs, e.g. swims, grows	☐	☐
• quantity adjectives, e.g. few, some, many	☐	☐
• classifying adjectives, e.g. **tropical** fish	☐	☐
• adverbs to describe action, e.g. fly **rapidly.**	☐	☐
TOTAL	☐	☐

Procedure – A procedure gives instructions on how to make or do something.

	Yes	No
Purpose: Does it tell the reader how to make or do something?	☐	☐
Structure: When I write a procedure, I include:		
• goal	☐	☐
• materials	☐	☐
• steps.	☐	☐
Forms: I can write:		
• a recipe	☐	☐
• instructions on how to make or do something	☐	☐
• the rules for a game	☐	☐
• directions.	☐	☐

	Yes	No
Grammar: I have used:		
• present-tense action verbs, e.g. climb	☐	☐
• adverbs e.g. carefully	☐	☐
• commands, e.g. Count the number of heartbeats.	☐	☐
• conjunctions, e.g. and, but, or	☐	☐
• time and sequence words, e.g. before	☐	☐
• factual adjectives about size, shape, colour.	☐	☐
TOTAL	☐	☐

Self-assessment

Exposition – An exposition consists of arguments from one or more points of view.

	Yes	No
Purpose: Does your text argue or persuade from one or more points of view?	☐	☐
Structure: When I write a persuasive text I include:		
• statement of position (my point of view)	☐	☐
• arguments for and/or against my point/points of view	☐	☐
• concluding statement (restatement of my point of view).	☐	☐
Forms: I can write:		
• an argument	☐	☐
• a discussion	☐	☐
• a persuasive poster.	☐	☐

	Yes	No
Grammar: I have used:		
• common nouns, e.g. adults, rubbish	☐	☐
• pronouns – personal and possessive	☐	☐
• present-tense verbs	☐	☐
• sensing verbs (to describe feelings), e.g. think, enjoy, wish	☐	☐
• relating verbs, e.g. am, is, can	☐	☐
• time words to link arguments, e.g. then, after.	☐	☐
TOTAL	☐	☐

Explanations – Explanations explain how and why things happen or how something works or has formed.

	Yes	No
Purpose: Does it explain how or why something has happened?	☐	☐
Structure: When I write an explanation, I include:		
• identifying statement	☐	☐
• explanation sequence	☐	☐
• summary statement.	☐	☐
Forms: I can write:		
• an explanation produced as a result of a question and research-based answers	☐	☐
• a flow chart or explanatory diagram	☐	☐

	Yes	No
Grammar: I have used:		
• technical nouns, e.g. earthquakes	☐	☐
• action verbs, e.g. vibrates, flows	☐	☐
• present tense, e.g. crashing	☐	☐
• adverbial phrases telling how, when, where	☐	☐
• text connectives that show cause and effect, e.g. because, if, when.	☐	☐
TOTAL	☐	☐

Narrative – A narrative tells a story or entertains readers by telling a series of events with a problem and a solution.

	Yes	No
Purpose: Does it tell a story or entertain?	☐	☐
Structure: When I write a narrative, I include:		
• an orientation telling who, what, where	☐	☐
• a complication, a problem	☐	☐
• resolution: the problem is solved.	☐	☐
Forms: I can write:		
• a story or play	☐	☐
• a myth, fable or legend.	☐	☐

	Yes	No
Grammar: I have used:		
• common and proper nouns	☐	☐
• personal and possessive pronouns	☐	☐
• adjectives	☐	☐
• past-tense verbs	☐	☐
• conjunctions	☐	☐
• time and sequence words	☐	☐
TOTAL	☐	☐

Self–assessment and reflection:

Cross-Reference Chart

Key
Unit number–**Page number**

Focus	Book 1	Book 2	Book 3	Book 4	Book 5	Book 6
Nouns – common	1–**6**, 2–**8**	1–**6**, 2–**8**	1–**6**	1–**6**	1–**6**, 4–**12**	1–**6**
Nouns – proper	4–**12**, 5–**14**	4–**12**, 5–**14**	2–**8**	2–**8**	2–**8**	2–**8**
Nouns – collective				4–**12**	3–**10**	4–**12**
Nouns – technical						3–**10**
Nouns – plurals	6–**16**	6–**16**	3–**10**, 13–**30**	3–**10**	6–**16**	5–**14**
Pronouns	10–**24**	10–**24**	14–**32**	5–**14**, 6–**16**	5–**14**	6–**16**
Adjectives	8–**20**, 9–**22**	8–**20**, 9–**22**	4–**12**, 5–**14**	7–**18**, 8–**20**	8–**20**, 9–**22**	8–**20**, 9–**22**
Verbs	11–**26**	11–**26**, 12–**28**	8–**20**, 9–**22**, 10–**24**	10–**24**, 11–**26**, 12–**28**	10–**24**, 11–**26**	10–**24**
Verb tense	12–**28**, 13–**30**				12–**28**	12–**28**
Adverbs	15–**34**	15–**34**	12–**28**	13–**30**, 14–**32**	15–**34**	13–**30**
Prepositions	16–**36**	16–**36**	16–**36**	23–**50**	16–**36**	15–**34**
Phrases		17–**38**		24–**52**	17–**38**	16–**36**
Conjunctions	22–**48**	25–**54**	15–**24**	22–**48**	18–**40**	17–**38**
Subject and predicate						18–**40**
Clauses				25–**54**	13–**30**	19–**42**
Simple sentences	17–**38**	18–**40**	11–**26**, 20–**44**		28–**60**	20–**44**
Compound sentences					28–**60**	20–**44**
Complex sentences					19–**42**	20–**44**
Statement		19–**42**			21–**46**, 29–**62**	23–**50**
Question	18–**40**	20–**44**	18–**40**	17–**38**	21–**46**, 29–**62**	23–**50**
Exclamation	19–**42**	21–**46**	19–**42**	18–**40**	21–**46**, 29–**62**	23–**50**
Command		13–**30**			29–**62**	11–**26**, 23–**50**
Full stops	3–**10**	3–**10**	6–**16**, 7–**18**		21–**46**	
Capital letters	3–**10**	3–**10**	6–**16**, 7–**18**			
Commas			21–**46**	16–**36**	22–**48**	
Apostrophe – of possession				19–**43**	23–**50**	24–**52**
Apostrophe – of contraction	20–**44**	28–**60**	17–**38**	19–**42**	24–**52**	25–**54**
Direct speech	27–**58**	27–**58**	22–**48**	20–**44**	25–**54**	26–**56**
Indirect speech						26–**56**
Paragraphs						22–**48**
Synonyms	23–**50**	23–**50**		30–**64**	27–**58**	28–**60**
Antonyms	24–**52**	24–**52**		29–**62**	27–**58**	28–**60**
Compound words	26–**56**	29–**62**				
Figurative language		30–**64**	29–**62**	27–**58**		29–**62**, 30–**64**
Alliteration	29–**62**	30–**64**	30–**64**	26–**56**		
Onomatopoeia	30–**64**	30–**64**		28–**60**		30–**64**
Metaphor						30–**64**
Review units	7–**18**, 14–**32**, 21–**46**, 28–**60**	7–**18**, 14–**32**, 22–**48**	23–**50**, 24–**52**, 25–**54**, 26–**56**, 27–**58**, 29–**62**	9–**15**, 15–**34**, 21–**46**	7–**18**, 14–**32**, 20–**44**, 26–**56**, 30–**64**	7–**18**, 14–**32**, 21–**46**, 27–**58**